Arthur R. Seymour

La Alhambra de Granada

SHORT
SPANISH REVIEW GRAMMAR
AND COMPOSITION BOOK

WITH EVERYDAY IDIOM DRILL
AND CONVERSATIONAL PRACTICE

BY

ARTHUR ROMEYN SEYMOUR
ASSOCIATE IN ROMANCE LANGUAGES

AND

DAVID HOBART CARNAHAN
PROFESSOR OF ROMANCE LANGUAGES
UNIVERSITY OF ILLINOIS

2d edition

D. C. HEATH AND COMPANY
BOSTON   NEW YORK   CHICAGO

PREFACE

THE purpose of this book is threefold: (*a*) to furnish a systematic review of the essentials of grammar in the second year of College work or in the third year of High School work; (*b*) to serve as a basal review in first-year College classes composed of students who have had Spanish in the High School; (*c*) to supply all the necessary material for a rapid-fire review at the beginning of an advanced course.

No attempt is made to teach the complicated grammatical or syntactical constructions of advanced composition. The grammatical material is strictly limited, in order not to confuse students with an excess of details. The object is to work over repeatedly the fundamental rules of grammar and to apply them to reading and composition of a lively, conversational style. Persistent drill leads the student to acquire a valuable practical equipment of useful Spanish.

Grammatical forms and colloquial idioms appear continually in different guise, so that the student should receive not only grammatical drill, but also practice in conversational Spanish. Besides the usual questions in Spanish based on the text, *temas* are provided to serve as a guide to oral narration or for conversation.

In order to stimulate interest, the lessons are based on the actual experiences of Americans traveling in Spain. Everyday events are described in everyday language.

Practical suggestions for overcoming the difficulties of the irregular verbs, tense by tense, are conveniently furnished near the beginning of the book. The Appendices contain a complete outline of the regular and irregular verbs, as well as reference lists of the irregular verbs and of those which govern an infinitive with or without certain prepositions.

The Spanish-English and English-Spanish vocabularies in synoptic form are an important element of the book. The arrangement of both on the same page affords a considerable saving of time.

Since the book is for intermediate students, the arrangement of the grammatical material differs frequently from that of elementary grammars. A few irregular verbs are given in complete form in each lesson. They are arranged, in general, according to frequency of use. The idioms have been chosen for their practical conversational value, and as far as feasible, employ the irregular verbs found in the same lesson.

The book may be finished in one semester by allowing two classroom periods a week to each of the fifteen lessons, but better results will be obtained by devoting more time to each lesson.

SUGGESTIONS TO TEACHERS

The authors are of the belief that there is no method which applies equally well to all conditions, and make the following suggestions with due reserve. In order to meet the necessities of different institutions, the following plans are proposed:

Plan I (Two class periods to one lesson).

First day: Grammar section, Section A, first half of Section C.
Second day: Section B (I) or B (II), second half of C, and Section D.

Plan II (Three class periods to one lesson).

No. 1.

First day: Grammar section, Section A.
Second day: Review A, Section B (I), first half of C.
Third day: Section B (II), second half of C, and D.

No. 2.

First day: Grammar section, first half of D.
Second day: Section A, B (I), first half of C.
Third day: Section B (II), second half of C, second half of D.

Plan III (Four class periods to one lesson).

First day: Grammar section.
Second day: Section A, and B (I).
Third day: Section B (II), first half of C.
Fourth day: Second half of C, and D.

NOTE (*important*): — Plan III can be used in a mixed course of literature and composition. Devote the first 20–30 minutes of four class periods to this book, using the rest of the period for literary work in another book.

Plan IV (For advanced classes).

One classroom period to one lesson.
Omit one or more sections, subject to the conditions of the class.

The authors wish to acknowledge their indebtedness to Professor E. C. Hills of the University of California, to Professor John Van Horne and Miss Adelaida Smithers of the University of Illinois, and to Dr. Alexander Green of D. C. Heath and Co. for their valuable help in the preparation of this book; as well as to Dr. Homero Serís, Presidente de la Unión Benéfica Española of New York City, and to Dr. Carlos C. Castillo of the University of Chicago, for their generous and helpful criticisms of the Spanish sections of the text.

A. R. S.
D. H. C.

URBANA, ILLINOIS,
June, 1923.

CONTENTS

CLASSROOM EXPRESSIONS

1. Buenos días, señor profesor. — Good morning, professor.
2. Buenas tardes, señorita. — Good afternoon, Miss.
3. Buenas noches, señora. — Good evening, Madam.
4. ¿Cómo está Vd. ? — How are you ?
5. Muy bien (bueno), **gracias**, ¿y Vd. ? — Very well, thank you. And how are you ?
6. Sin novedad. — As usual.
7. Adiós. — Goodbye.
8. Hasta luego (mañana). — See you later (to-morrow).
9. Voy a pasar lista. — I am going to call the roll.
10. ¿Qué lección tenemos hoy ? — What lesson do we have to-day ?
11. Tenemos la lección quince. — We have lesson fifteen.
12. ¿En qué página ? — On what page ?
13. ¿Qué línea (renglón) ? — What line ?
14. La lectura empieza en la página veinte. — The reading begins on page twenty.
15. Esta es la lección para mañana. — This is the lesson for to-morrow.
16. Al principio de la página. — At the beginning of the page.
17. En el medio de la página. — In the middle of the page.
18. Al pie de la página. — At the bottom of the page.
19. Sírvase Vd. hacerme preguntas. — Please ask me questions.
20. Se debe decir. — You must say.
21. Abra Vd. el libro. — Open the book.
22. Cierre Vd. el libro. — Close the book.
23. Lea Vd. el español. — Read the Spanish.
24. Siga Vd. leyendo. — Go on reading.
25. Principie Vd. la traducción. — Begin the translation.
26. Traduzca Vd. al español. — Translate into Spanish.
27. Repítalo Vd. — Repeat it.
28. ¿Cómo se dice eso en español ? — How do you say that in Spanish ?
29. ¿Cómo se llama esto ? — What is the name of this ?
30. ¿Qué quiere decir esto ? — What does this mean ?
31. No sé lo que quiere decir. — I don't know what it means.
32. Fíjese Vd. en eso. — Pay attention to that.
33. Está bien. — All right, it is correct.
34. Está en el vocabulario. — It is in the vocabulary.
35. Pase Vd. a la pizarra (al pizarrón). — Go to the blackboard.
36. No hay tiza. — There is no chalk.
37. Aquí está el cepillo. — Here is the eraser.
38. Borre Vd. lo escrito. — Erase what is written.
39. Corrija Vd. las oraciones. — Correct the sentences.
40. Copie Vd. el ejercicio. — Copy the exercise.
41. Escríbalo Vd. en el cuaderno. — Write it in your notebook.
42. ¿Cómo se escribe esa palabra ? — How is that word written (spelled) ?

GRAMMATICAL TERMS

adjetivo *m.*	adjective
adverbio *m.*	adverb
complemento *m.*	object
directo	direct
indirecto	indirect
conjugación *f.*	conjugation
conjunción *f.*	conjunction
género *m.*	gender
masculino	masculine
femenino	feminine
neutro	neuter
gerundio *m.*	present participle
infinitivo *m.*	infinitive
interjección *f.*	interjection
modo *m.*	mood
imperativo	imperative
indicativo	indicative
subjuntivo	subjunctive
nombre (sustantivo) *m.*	noun
número *m.*	number
singular	singular
plural	plural
partes de la oración *f. pl.*	parts of speech
participio pasivo *m.*	past participle
persona *f.*	person
primera	first
segunda	second
tercera	third
preposición *f.*	preposition
pronombre	pronoun
demostrativo	demonstrative
interrogativo	interrogative
personal	personal
posesivo	possessive
relativo	relative
sujeto *m.*	subject
tiempo *m.*	tense
condicional	conditional
futuro	future
imperfecto	imperfect
perfecto	perfect (present perfect)
pluscuamperfecto	pluperfect
presente	present
pretérito	preterite
pretérito perfecto	past anterior
verbo *m.*	verb
auxiliar	auxiliary
reflexivo	reflexive

SPANISH REVIEW GRAMMAR

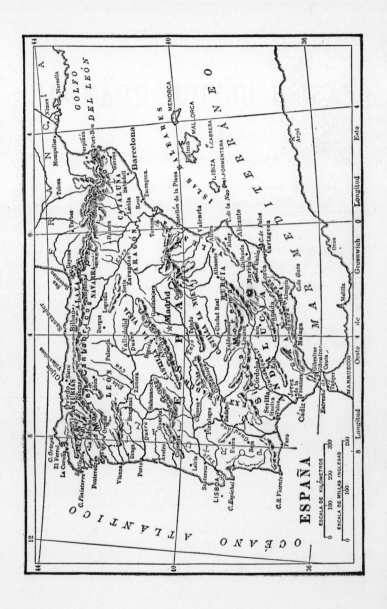

ESPAÑA

SPANISH REVIEW GRAMMAR

The Articles (I) — *Haber* and *Tener*

1. Definite and indefinite articles. — The following is the table of definite and indefinite articles:

	Masculine		Feminine		Neuter
	SINGULAR	PLURAL	SINGULAR	PLURAL	SINGULAR
Definite:	el	los	la[2]	las	lo[3]
Indefinite:	un	unos[4]	una	unas	

(a) **de + el** becomes **del** (*of the, from the*)

a + el becomes **al** (*to the, at the, etc.*)

2. Agreement. — Articles must agree with their nouns in gender and number, and are ordinarily repeated before each noun to which they refer.

Las universidades de los Estados Unidos son grandes.
The universities of the United States are large.

El té, el café, y la leche están en la mesa.
The tea, coffee and milk are on the table.

El (Un) hombre y la (una) mujer están en el automóvil.
The (A) man and woman are in the automobile.

---

[1] For discussion of teaching methods, see Preface.

[2] **El** is used instead of **la** before a feminine noun beginning with stressed **a** or **ha**, unless an adjective intervenes. **El agua,** *the water.* BUT: **La buena agua,** *the good water.*

[3] The neuter article, **lo,** is used chiefly before adjectives and past participles used as nouns, and occasionally before adverbs. **Lo bueno y lo malo,** *good and evil.* **Lo escrito,** *what is written.* **A lo lejos,** *in the distance.* See § **26.**

[4] The forms **unos** and **unas** mean *some, a few.* **Algunos, -as** may also be so used.

3

3. Use of the definite article. — The definite article is used in Spanish when it is not required in English:[1]

1. Before a noun used in a general or inclusive sense (collective and abstract nouns, etc.).

El hierro es duro.	Iron is hard.
Todo el mundo desea la libertad.	Everybody desires liberty.

2. Before infinitives used as verbal nouns.

El comer es necesario.	Eating is necessary.
Al encontrarme, me saludó cortésmente.	Upon meeting me, he greeted me courteously.
BUT: Es necesario comer.	It is necessary to eat.

3. Before the names of the days of the week, the seasons, and with expressions of time when modified by **próximo, pasado,** etc.

Saldrá de Cádiz el lunes.	He will leave Cadiz on[2] Monday.
Llueve mucho en la primavera.	It rains much in spring.
Mi hermano vino la semana pasada.	My brother came last week.

4. Before titles[3] preceding proper names, except in direct address.

El general Valdés está en Madrid.	General Valdés is in Madrid.
El señor García lo dijo.	Mr. García said so.
BUT: Buenos días, señor García.	Good morning, Mr. García.

5. Before the names of geographical divisions (continents, countries, etc.) when modified by an adjective or adjectival

---

[1] For the use of the definite article instead of the possessive adjective, see § **97**; instead of the demonstrative pronoun, see § **111.**

[2] For the omission of *on* before the days of the week, see § **60,** 1, footnote 1.

[3] The titles **don** and **doña** (used before given names only) do not require the article before them. **Don Roberto y doña María están aquí,** *Mr. Robert and Miss Mary are here.*

phrase. The names of certain countries and cities regularly
require the article, such as: **el Brasil, el Canadá, el Perú,**[1]
la Coruña. Unmodified names, with the exception of the
last mentioned group, ordinarily do not require the article.

La España antigua tiene una historia interesante.	Ancient Spain has an interesting history.
BUT: **España es interesante.**	Spain is interesting.
Jorge está en la América del Sur.	George is in South America.
El Perú tiene muchas minas de plata.	Peru has many silver mines.
Salgo de Cuba para España.	I am leaving Cuba for Spain.

6. Before the name of a language. However it is not
used directly after **hablar,**[2] nor ordinarily in phrases beginning with **de** or **en.**

El español es un idioma muy musical.	Spanish is a very musical language.
Hablamos español en la clase de español.	We speak Spanish in the Spanish class.
Escribí una carta en español.	I wrote a Spanish letter.

7. Before nouns of weight and measure, instead of the
indefinite article.

Costó tres pesetas el metro.	It cost three pesetas a meter.
Pagaré dos pesetas la libra.	I shall pay two pesetas a pound.

4. *Haber.* — The verb **haber** is used: —

1. As an auxiliary in order to form the compound tenses.[3]

He comprado [4] **una bicicleta.**	I have bought a bicycle.
Habían escrito las cartas.	They had written the letters.

---

[1] Other American countries, the names of which require the article are:
el Ecuador, las Guayanas, el Paraguay, el Uruguay, (la) Argentina, los Estados Unidos.

[2] **El castellano,** sometimes used instead of **español** with the meaning of
Spanish language, requires the article even after **hablar.**

[3] In compound tenses with **haber** the past participle does not vary in
ending. See § **170.**

[4] Note also that, differing from English and French usage, no word may
come between forms of **haber** and the past participle, except a personal

2. As an impersonal verb (*in the third person singular only*) with the meaning of *there is, there are, there was, there were,* etc. The special form **hay** is used in the present indicative.

Hay españoles en la clase.	There are Spaniards in the class.
Habrá bastante tiempo mañana.	There will be plenty of time to-morrow.

5. *Tener.* — The verb **tener**[1] ordinarily means *to have,* in the sense of *to possess.*

Tuvimos muchos libros.	We had many books.
¿ Tiene Vd. mi paraguas ?	Have you my umbrella?

VERBS[2]

6.   Haber, *to have*

Pres. Part. habiendo; Past Part. habido.
Pres. Ind. he,[3] has, ha, hemos, habéis, han.
Pres. Subj. haya, hayas, haya, hayamos, hayáis, hayan.
Impf. Ind. había, etc.; Fut. Ind. habré, etc.; Cond. habría, etc.
Pret. Ind. hube, hubiste, hubo, hubimos, hubisteis, hubieron.
Impf. Subjs. hubiese, etc.; hubiera, etc.; Fut. Subj. hubiere, etc.

7.   Tener, *to have*

Pres. Part. teniendo; Past Part. tenido.
Pres. Ind. tengo, tienes, tiene, tenemos, tenéis, tienen.

---

pronoun object when used after the infinitive or present participle of **haber**. **No he leído nunca la revista,** *I have never read the magazine.* **Habiéndonos visto, salió,** *Having seen us, he went out.*

[1] **Tener** may be followed by the past participle used adjectively to indicate a state or condition of affairs, rather than an action. **Tengo abierta la ventana,** *I have the window open* (condition). But: **He abierto la ventana,** *I have opened the window* (action).

[2] For rules of verb formation, see Supplement to Exercise I, and Appendix B.

[3] Note that the infinitives and the irregular forms are in black-faced type.

PRES. SUBJ. **tenga, tengas, tenga, tengamos, tengáis, tengan.**
IMPF. IND. **tenía,** etc.; FUT. IND. **tendré,** etc.; COND. **tendría,** etc.
PRET. IND. **tuve, tuviste, tuvo, tuvimos, tuvisteis, tuvieron.**
IMPF. SUBJS. **tuviese,** etc.; **tuviera,** etc.; FUT. SUBJ. **tuviere,** etc.
IMPERATIVES **ten,** tened.

IDIOMS

8. *Haber que* (+ *infinitive*).   To be necessary (*used impersonally*)

Hay que ir a España.   It is necessary to go to Spain.

9. *Tener que* (+ *infinitive*).   To have to, must

Tengo que escribir una carta.   I have to (must) write a letter.

10. *Tener* in other idioms: —

Tener calor[1]	To be warm	*Tener sueño*	To be sleepy
Tener frío	To be cold	*Tener . . . años*	To be. . .years old
Tener hambre	To be hungry	*Tener miedo* (*de*)	To be afraid (of)
Tener sed	To be thirsty	*Tener cuidado* (*de*)	To be careful (of)
Tener razón	To be right	*Tener vergüenza* (*de*)	To be ashamed(of)
No tener razón	To be wrong	*Tener gana*(*s*) (*de*)	To feel like, be desirous (of)

Tener las manos frías, etc.	To have cold hands, etc.
Tener mucho gusto en	To be very glad to
Tenemos mucho frío en el invierno.	We are very cold in winter.
¿ Cuántos años tiene Vd. ?	How old are you?
Tuvo miedo de caer.	He was afraid of falling.
Tengo los ojos cansados.	My eyes are tired.
Tuvimos mucho gusto en hacerlo.	We were very glad to do it.

---

[1] This list of idioms is used with persons and animals but not with things.

A

Algeciras, España.
15 de junio de 19—

Querido Alberto:

Con mucho gusto me hallo al fin en España. He llegado
hoy a Algeciras, en el sur de España, y tengo muchas ganas
de escribirle una carta en español. Al salir del puerto de
5 Nueva York para España, y al ver desaparecer a lo lejos la
famosa estatua de la Libertad, me sentí como un explorador
que va a aventurarse en un nuevo mundo. El viajar en el
verano, sobre todo en el mes de junio, es muy ameno, porque
entonces el Atlántico está casi siempre tranquilo. No hay
10 que tener tanto cuidado de la salud como en el invierno. No
tenía miedo de marearme.

Mis mejores amigos entre los pasajeros eran el señor
Carlos López y el señor Roberto Gómez, naturales de España,
quienes volvían a su patria para pasar unas semanas del
15 verano entre las escenas de la juventud. Apenas hay que
decirle que siempre hablábamos español en el vapor. Me
encantó el entusiasmo de mis dos amigos al hablar de España
que es una tierra muy rica en lo histórico y en lo romántico.
Tengo que visitar las ciudades, los museos, las corridas y
20 los teatros de los cuales me han hablado tanto. Don Carlos
y don Roberto han prometido ayudarme, al llegar yo a sus
ciudades natales. Don Roberto es granadino y don Carlos
madrileño.

No tengo ganas de marcharme de este hotel tan hermoso
25 y tan moderno en el cual me encuentro. Las flores del jardín
delante del hotel son magníficas, y prueban que el sur de
España tiene un clima favorable para las flores. La lluvia
no es abundante, y por eso hay que regar las flores casi todos
los días. Don Roberto tenía razón en celebrar el clima del
30 sur de su patria. Es verdad que tengo calor esta tarde,
pero no importa. Hoy está tan transparente el aire que veo

distintamente a lo lejos el gran peñón de Gibraltar al otro lado de la bahía.

Ahora hay que bajar para la comida, y de veras tengo mucha hambre. Estoy muy contento, porque ya tengo escrita mi primera carta desde España. Recuerdos a todos 5 los amigos.

Su afmo. amigo
Luis

B

I. *Cuestionario*

1. ¿ Cuándo llegó Luis a España? 2. ¿ A qué ciudad llegó? 3. ¿ Qué vió al salir de Nueva York? 4. ¿ Cuándo es mejor viajar, y por qué? 5. ¿ Qué idioma hablaban los amigos en el vapor? 6. ¿ Qué tiene que visitar Luis en España? 7. ¿ Quiénes le ayudarán durante sus viajes por España? 8. ¿ Por qué no tenía ganas de marcharse del hotel? 9. ¿ Qué hay que hacer con las flores ? 10. ¿ Qué vió Luis al otro lado de la bahía?

II. *Temas*

1. La llegada a España.
2. La estatua de la Libertad.
3. El viajar por el Atlántico.
4. Los tres amigos en el vapor.
5. Las cosas que hay que ver en España.
6. Un hotel moderno.
7. El jardín del hotel.
8. El clima del sur de España.
9. El peñón de Gibraltar.
10. La comida.

C

(JOHN *and* LOUIS, *two students from America, have come to Spain to*[1] *travel and to learn Spanish.*)

JOHN (*in Louis's*[2] *room in a hotel at*[3] *Algeciras*). — Good morning, Mr. Traveler, are you still sleepy? Do you not

---

[1] **Para** (§ 112). For lists of verbs requiring the direct infinitive or certain prepositions, see Lesson XV or Appendix D.

[2] *The room of Louis.* [3] **en.**

feel like going downstairs[1] for[2] breakfast? Your eyes are
tired; you[3] will have to go to bed early to-night. Can you
not hurry? I am hungry.

Louis. — You are always hungry. " Patience is an
5 excellent virtue." Have you forgotten that Professor
Álvarez used to say to us in the Spanish class, especially on
Mondays, " Patience, gentlemen, accomplishes everything;
but, unfortunately, youth is lazy. Are you not ashamed to
pass Saturday and Sunday without working[4] ? " Then he
10 used to say, " Spanish is not hard for Americans,[5] nor
for Englishmen, if they can[6] visit Spain[7] or South America.[7]
Likewise, Spaniards can learn English easily in England.
I learned English easily."

John. — Professor Álvarez is wrong sometimes. He is
15 forty years old, and has passed several years in England and
in North America, and nevertheless he does not speak
English very well . . . I have to leave Algeciras to-day.
General Gómez, my friend who lives in South America and
who arrived from France on June 10th, will be in Spain
20 next week, and I have to see him at Granada.

Louis. — Well, I am very glad to go downstairs now.
I know well that you are hungry. Eating is very important.
You had an enormous appetite on the boat.

John. — There are many travelers on the boats in spring
25 and summer, and the meals are good, especially on Sundays
and Wednesdays. There was wine on the table, but I drank
the water. I was afraid of being seasick. I do not like[8] the
Atlantic; I like the Mediterranean better.[9]

---

[1] *go downstairs* = **bajar.**   [2] **Para** (§112).   [3] Omit, (§ 72).
[4] Infin. (§ 161).   [5] American (*of U. S. A.*) = **norteamericano.**
[6] Indicative, (§ 151, *a*). [7] Use **a** (§ 38). [8] **no me gusta.** [9] **más.**

D

Drill

1. Charles, Professor Álvarez has already come. 2. I haven't studied my lesson; I didn't feel like studying on Saturday. 3. Are you not ashamed? Studying is a pleasure. 4. Why are you always sleepy on Mondays, especially in spring and in autumn? 5. Good morning, Professor,[1] Charles and I were studying Spanish. 6. My uncle says that southern Spain has a climate favorable for flowers, especially in spring. 7. Are there flowers in Spain in winter? 8. I have to go to Spain or to South America next summer. 9. If Spaniards are[2] cold in winter, they have to go to the Mediterranean. 10. Robert's[3] friend was warm and thirsty. 11. I shall be very glad to arrive at Algeciras. 12. We shall be careful to speak Spanish. 13. They will have to remain on the steamer. 14. I was thirsty, and I had to drink the warm water. 15. There will be some flowers on the table; they cost five pesetas a dozen. 16. We have two windows open; my feet are cold. 17. How old is she? She is fifteen years old. 18. He used to be afraid of being seasick. 19. It will be necessary to[4] go to Peru on the fourth of May. 20. Who has said, "Liberty or death?"

---

[1] señor profesor.
[3] *the friend of Robert.*
[2] Indicative (§ **151,** *a*).
[4] No preposition (§ **163**)

SUPPLEMENT TO EXERCISE I (VERB FORMATION)

A. RADICAL-CHANGING VERBS

Class I (-*ar* and -*er* verbs)

STRESSED SYLLABLE

e >ie ⎰ Pres. Ind. 1st, 2d, 3rd sing., 3rd pl.
o >ue ⎱ Pres. Subj. 1st, 2d, 3rd sing., 3rd pl.
⎩ Imperative 2d sing.

Typical verbs: pensar — pienso, etc.; contar — cuento, etc.; perder — pierdo, etc.; volver — vuelvo, etc.

(*a*) Initial o >ue >hue: oler — huelo, etc.

Initial e >ie >ye: errar — yerro, etc.

Class II (-*ir* verbs)

STRESSED SYLLABLE	UNSTRESSED SYLLABLE
(*Same changes as in Class I*)	Pres. Part.
e >ie ⎰ Pres. Ind. 1st, 2d, 3rd sing., 3rd pl.	e >i Pres. Subj. 1st, 2d pl.
o >ue ⎱ Pres. Subj. 1st, 2d, 3rd sing., 3rd pl.	o >u Pret. Ind. 3rd sing., 3rd pl.
⎩ Imperative 2d sing.	-se Impf. Subj. ⎱ all -ra Impf. Subj. ⎰ six Fut. Subj. forms

Typical verbs: sentir — siento, etc.; dormir — duermo, etc.; sentir — sintiendo, etc.; dormir — durmiendo, etc.

Class III (-*ir* verbs)

STRESSED SYLLABLE	UNSTRESSED SYLLABLE
(*Same forms changed as in Class I, but the change is different*)	Pres. Part.
e >i ⎰ Pres. Ind. 1st, 2d, 3rd sing., 3rd pl.	e >i Pres. Subj. 1st, 2d pl.
Pres. Subj. 1st, 2d, 3rd sing., 3rd pl.	Pret. Ind. 3rd sing., 3rd pl.
⎩ Imperative 2d sing.	-se Impf. Subj. ⎱ all -ra Impf. Subj. ⎰ six Fut. Subj. forms

Typical verb: pedir — pido, etc.; pedir — pidiendo, etc.

B. ORTHOGRAPHIC-CHANGING VERBS

I. Changes which preserve the consonantal sound found in the infinitive.[1]

1. *Before* **e** (*of ending*)

-car	c > qu	Pret. Ind. 1st sing.	
-gar	g > gu		all
-guar	gu > gü	Pres. Subj.	six
-zar	z > c		forms

2. *Before* **a** *or* **o** (*of ending*)

-cer ⎱	cons. c > z	Pres. Ind. 1st sing.	
-cir ⎰	vow. c > zc	Pres. Ind. 1st sing.	
-ger ⎰			
-gir ⎱	g > j		all
-guir	gu > g	Pres. Subj.	six
-quir	qu > c		forms

Typical verbs: (1) tocar — toqué, etc.; pagar — pagué, etc.; averiguar — averigüé, etc.; gozar — gocé, etc.; (2) vencer — venzo, etc.; esparcir — esparzo, etc.; conocer — conozco, etc.; lucir — luzco, etc.; coger — cojo, etc.; dirigir — dirijo, etc.; distinguir — distingo, etc.; delinquir — delinco, etc.

II. *Y* and *I* changes.

1. In **-uír** verbs (not **-guir** and **-quir**) **y** is inserted at the end of the stem. (In 1st, 2d, 3rd sing., 3rd pl. of the Pres. Ind. and Pres. Subj., and in the Imperative 2d sing.). Huír — huyo, etc.

2. The **i** of the regular endings **-ie** and **-ió** becomes **y** when the stem of the verb ends in a vowel. (In Pres. Part., 3rd sing., 3rd pl. Pret. and all of the forms of the **-se** Impf. Subj., **-ra** Impf. Subj., and Fut. Subj.). Leer — leyendo, etc. (But **-ii** becomes **i**. Reír — riendo, etc.).

3. The **i** of the regular ending is lost when the stem ends in ll, ñ, and j. (In Pret. Ind. 3rd sing., 3rd pl. and all forms of the **-se** Impf. Subj., **-ra** Impf. Subj., and Fut. Subj. *Also,* in ll and ñ verbs in Pres. Part.) Bullir — bulleron, etc.; reñir — riñeron, etc.; decir — dijeron, etc.

---

[1] With the exception of the **c** — **zc** group.

C. DRILL ON VERB FORMS

Radical Changes

The following verbs are used in the exercise below: **pensar,** *think;* **contar,** *count;* **perder,** *lose;* **volver,** *return;* **sentir,** *feel;* **dormir,** *sleep;* **pedir,** *ask.* Translate into Spanish:

1. I ask. 2. They felt. 3. You [1] lose. 4. They slept. 5. That they may think (*pres. subj.*). 6. We lose. 7. They count. 8. You (*pl.*) ask. 9. Sleep (*imperative sing.*). 10. We think. 11. Let us ask (*pres. subj.*). 12. They return. 13. That he may lose (*pres. subj.*). 14. I asked. 15. She thinks. 16. You count. 17. He feels. 18. We return. 19. You (*pl.*) asked. 20. That they might feel (*impf. subj.*). 21. Let us count (*pres subj.*). 22. I think. 23. That he may return (*pres. subj.*). 24. We slept. 25. I lose. 26. That they may count (*pres. subj.*). 27. That you may think (*pres. subj.*). 28. You (*pl.*) feel. 29. Let us sleep (*pres. subj.*). 30. I count. 31. That I may lose (*pres. subj.*). 32. We felt. 33. That they might sleep (*impf. subj.*). 34. She felt. 35. I return.

Orthographic Changes

I. The following verbs are used in the exercise below: **tocar,** *touch;* **pagar,** *pay;* **averiguar,** *ascertain;* **gozar,** *enjoy;* **vencer,** *conquer;* **esparcir,** *scatter;* **conocer,** *know;* **lucir,** *shine;* **coger,** *catch;* **dirigir,** *direct;* **distinguir,** *distinguish;* **delinquir,** *transgress.* Translate into Spanish:

1. I know. 2. Let us catch (*pres. subj.*). 3. That you may direct (*pres. subj.*). 4. It shines. 5. That you (*pl.*) may enjoy (*pres. subj.*). 6. I touched. 7. I distinguish. 8. That they may transgress (*pres. subj.*). 9. They catch. 10. Let us touch (*pres. subj.*). 11. I ascertained. 12. That it may shine (*pres. subj.*). 13. They conquer. 14. That we may pay (*pres. subj.*). 15. I scatter. 16. He distinguishes. 17. That they may shine (*pres. subj.*). 18. We direct. 19. I transgress. 20. That he may distinguish (*pres. subj.*). 21. They pay. 22. We ascertain. 23. I conquer. 24. He touched. 25. I direct. 26. They

---

[1] In these exercises translate you by **usted** and **ustedes.**

'ital.

transgress. 27. That they may scatter (*pres. subj.*). 28. I paid. 29. We enjoy. 30. That you may know (*pres. subj.*). 31. I catch. 32. Let us conquer (*pres. subj.*). 33. I enjoyed. 34. That they may ascertain (*pres. subj.*). 35. You scatter. 36. They know.

II. The following verbs are used in the exercise below: **huír,** *flee;* **leer,** *read;* **reír,** *laugh;* **bullir,** *boil;* **reñir,** *scold;* **decir,** *say.* Translate into Spanish:

1. He read. 2. Let us flee (*pres. subj.*). 3. It boiled. 4. They laughed. 5. That they might say (*impf. subj.*). 6. He scolded. 7. That they might read (*impf. subj.*). 8. Fleeing. 9. That we might laugh (*impf. subj.*). 10. Boiling. 11. They said. 12. Reading. 13. He fled. 14. She laughed. 15. Scolding. 16. He said.

D. GENERAL SUGGESTIONS

I. Present indicative.

1. When the first person singular present indicative has a consonantal change in the stem (also, with **dar** and **saber**), the remaining forms of the tense are regular.

Hacer — **hago, haces, hace, hacemos, hacéis, hacen.**

(*a*) The following verbs are exceptions: **decir, oír, tener, venir.**

2. The first and second persons plural of the present indicative are regular in *all* verbs except **ser — somos, sois; ir — vamos, vais; haber — hemos.**

II. Present subjunctive.

When the first person singular present indicative of any verb has a consonantal change in the stem, the present subjunctive has the same change in all six forms.

Hacer — **haga, hagas, haga, hagamos, hagáis, hagan.**

III. Imperative.

1. The imperative singular is the same as the third person singular present indicative. The following verbs are excep-

tions: poner — pon; salir — sal; tener — ten; venir —ven; valer — val(e); hacer — haz; decir — di; ir — ve; ser — sé.

2. The imperative plural may be obtained by changing the -r of the infinitive ending to -d. Venir — venid. (*No exceptions.*)

IV. Imperfect indicative.

This tense is regular in *all* verbs except ser — era, etc.; ir — iba, etc.; ver — veía, etc.

V. Future and conditional indicative.

These tenses are regular in most verbs. The verbs which are irregular in these tenses are:

1. Those that lose the vowel of the infinitive ending: haber — habré, habría; caber — cabré, cabría; poder — podré, podría; querer — querré, querría; saber — sabré, sabría.

2. Those that lose the vowel of the infinitive ending and insert d: poner — pondré, pondría; salir — saldré, saldría; tener — tendré, tendría; valer — valdré, valdría; venir — vendré, vendría.

3. Two verbs: decir — diré, diría; hacer — haré, haría.

VI. Preterite indicative.

All six forms of this tense are irregular in the following verbs:

1. Verbs in -ar: andar — anduve; dar — di; estar — estuve.

2. Verbs in -er: caber — cupe; haber — hube; hacer — hice; poder — pude; poner — puse; querer — quise; saber — supe; tener — tuve; ser — fuí.

3. Verbs in -ir: decir — dije; (-)ducir — (-)duje; venir — vine; ir — fuí.[1]

---

[1] With the exception of the verbs **dar, ser** and **ir,** all the verbs having irregular preterites have an unstressed -e in the first person singular and an unstressed -o in the third person singular.

VII. *-se* and *-ra* imperfect subjunctive and future subjunctive.

These tenses may be obtained by adding to the stem of the third person singular or plural of the preterite the following endings: -se Impf., -iese, etc.; -ra Impf., -iera, etc. Fut., -iere, etc. Example: quiso, quis-iese, etc.

(*a*) Exceptions without -i in the ending: decir — dijese, etc.; (-)ducir — (-)dujese, etc.; traer — trajese, etc.; ser — fuese, etc.; ir — fuese, etc.

VIII. Past participle.

1. Verbs in -ir and -er which are irregular in the past participle only: abrir — abierto; cubrir — cubierto; escribir — escrito; imprimir — impreso; prender — preso; romper — roto.

2. Other verbs having irregular past participles: decir — dicho; hacer — hecho; morir — muerto; poner — puesto; solver — suelto; ver — visto; volver — vuelto.

EXERCISE II

The Articles (II) — *Ser* and *Estar*

11. Omission of the Articles. — The definite and indefinite articles are not required before nouns in parenthetical apposition.[1]

Madrid, capital de España.	Madrid, the capital of Spain.
Alfonso X, rey de España.	Alfonso X, the (a) king of Spain.

12. The **indefinite article** is not required: —

1. Before an unmodified predicate noun expressing nationality, occupation, profession, etc.

No es cubano, es mejicano.	He is not a Cuban, he is a Mexican.
Soy médico, no soy ingeniero.	I am a doctor, I am not an engineer.
But: **Es un buen médico** (*modified*).	He is a good doctor.

2. Before **ciento**, *a (one) hundred*, **mil**, *a (one) thousand*, **otro**, *another*, **cierto**, *a certain*, after **qué**, *what a*, in exclamations, and after **tal**, *such a*.

Mil ciento veinte.	One thousand one hundred and twenty.
¡ Qué caballo (tan) hermoso !	What a beautiful horse !
Tal cosa me sorprendería.	Such a thing would surprise me.

13. *Ser.* — Uses of the verb **ser** [2] : —

---

[1] The definite article is used, nevertheless, with nouns in apposition, when they are used for the sake of identification. **Mi hermano, el médico, ha llegado,** *My brother, the doctor, has arrived.*

[2] For the use of **ser** in the passive voice, see § **133.**

1. With adjectives to express an inherent or characteristic quality (including age, appearance, character, and financial condition).

Aquel señor es viejo.	That gentleman is old.
La niña es bonita.	The girl is pretty.
Estos hombres son buenos, pero no son ricos.	These men are good, but they are not rich.

2. With a predicate noun or pronoun.

Era carpintero.	He was a carpenter.
Es ella.	It is she.

3. In impersonal expressions.

Es verdad.	It is true.
Es necesario hablar despacio.	It is necessary to speak slowly.

4. To express origin, ownership, and material.

Los comerciantes son de Barcelona.	The merchants are from Barcelona.
La guitarra es de mi prima.	The guitar is my cousin's.
Las corbatas eran de seda.	The neckties were silk.

5. To express the time of day.

¿ Qué hora es ? — Son las tres.	What time is it ? It is three o'clock.

14. *Estar.* — Uses of the verb **estar:** —

1. With adjectives to express a temporary state or condition.[1]

¿ Cómo está Vd. ? — Estoy bueno,[2] gracias.	How are you ? I am well, thank you.
La taza estaba llena.	The cup was full.
El agua está fría.	The water is (*temporarily*) cold.
BUT: El hielo es frío.	The ice is (*inherently*) cold.

---

[1] Certain adjectives have one meaning when used with **ser,** and another meaning when used with **estar. Está bueno,** *he is well;* **es bueno,** *he is good.* **Está malo,** *he is ill;* **es malo,** *he is bad.* **Está cansado,** *he is tired;* **es cansado,** *he is tiresome.*

[2] **Bien** may also be used, especially in the expression **muy bien.**

Conorete - hormigón

2. To express location (permanent as well as temporary).

Mi casa está en el campo.   My house is in the country.

Sus hermanos estuvieron en la tienda.   His brothers were in the store.

3. With the present participle to express continued or progressive action.

> **Nuestra hermana estaba estudiando toda la tarde.**
> Our sister was (*or* kept) studying all the afternoon.

4. With the past participle used as an adjective to express a state or condition of affairs, rather than an action. In this usage the past participle varies for gender and number.

> **Las puertas están cerradas.**   The doors are closed.

VERBS

15.   Ser, *to be*

PRES. PART. **siendo**; PAST PART. **sido.**

PRES. IND. **soy, eres, es, somos, sois, son.**

PRES. SUBJ. **sea, seas, sea, seamos, seáis, sean.**

IMPF. IND. **era, eras, era, éramos, erais, eran.**

FUT. IND. **seré,** etc.; COND. **sería,** etc.

PRET. IND. **fuí, fuiste, fué, fuimos, fuisteis, fueron.**

IMPF. SUBJS. **fuese,** etc.; **fuera,** etc.; FUT. SUBJ. **fuere,** etc.

IMPERATIVES **sé, sed.**

16.   Estar, *to be*

PRES. PART. **estando**; PAST PART. **estado.**

PRES. IND. **estoy, estás, está, estamos, estáis, están.**

PRES. SUBJ. **esté, estés, esté, estemos, estéis, estén.**

IMPF. IND. **estaba,** etc.; FUT. IND. **estaré,** etc.; COND. **estaría,** etc.

PRET. IND. **estuve, estuviste, estuvo, estuvimos, estuvisteis, estuvieron.**

IMPF. SUBJS. **estuviese,** etc.; **estuviera,** etc.; FUT. SUBJ. **estuviere** etc.

IMPERATIVES **está, estad.**

IDIOMS

17. *Acabar de* (+ *infinitive*) [1]   To have just (+ *past participle*)

Acaban de comprar unas flores.

They have just bought some flowers.

18. *Tratar de* (+ *infinitive*)   To try to

Trataban de aprender los modismos.

They were trying to learn the idioms.

19. *Cerca de*   Near

Estuvimos cerca de la puerta.

We were near the door.

A

Ronda, 20 de junio de 19—.

Querido Alberto:

Acabo de llegar a Ronda, ciudad interesante de la España meridional. Trataré de escribirle lo que sucedió ayer en el tren. Eran las nueve de la mañana cuando el tren salió de Algeciras. Naturalmente yo estaba sentado cerca de la 5 ventanilla para ver todo lo nuevo. Me encantaron los alcornoques, los olivos, las adelfas de los barrancos, y las aldeas pintorescas en las sierras.

Había otros dos pasajeros en el mismo compartimiento. Por lo que decían aprendí que uno era comerciante y el 10 otro era abogado. Estaban hablando todo el tiempo. Eran españoles y eran de Sevilla. Habían estado en Gibraltar y en Algeciras. Fueron muy bondadosos, y tuvieron cuidado de enseñarme las cosas de interés en el paisaje. Al fin tuve sed, y bajé en cierta estación para buscar agua. Compré 15 a un aguador un vaso de agua. El agua era buena, pero no estaba fría.

De pronto un empleado gritó: —¡ Señores viajeros al

---

[1] This use of **acabar** is restricted to the present and imperfect tenses.

tren! — Subí al tren.   Otro pasajero acababa de entrar en
nuestro compartimiento.   Llevaba tal cantidad de paquetes
que tuve miedo de no poder sentarme.   Fué necesario
tener mucho cuidado.   Este pasajero era viejo, y estaba
5 muy cansado como era de esperar.   ¡ Qué cantidad de
paquetes ! — ¿ Hasta dónde viaja Vd. ? — le preguntó uno de
los sevillanos. — Hasta Ronda — contestó el viejo. — Mi
hijo está allí.   Todos los paquetes son para él.   Esta caja
es de él, y está bastante pesada, porque contiene unas herra-
10 mientas de carpintero.   Mi hijo es carpintero, y quiso ir a
trabajar en Ronda, ciudad en donde puede ganar más
dinero que en nuestra aldea.   Somos pobres, y nos es
necesario trabajar para ganar la vida.

Al llegar el tren a Ronda, el hijo del viejo estaba en el
15 andén, y el viejo se le echó en los brazos. — Padre mío,
parece que estás malo, — dijo el hijo.   — ¡ Qué lástima !
— No, no estoy malo, pero estoy un poco cansado del
viaje. — Me despedí de mis compañeros que quedaban en el
tren, y bajé para ir a una fonda de la ciudad.   Pronto tendré
20 el gusto de escribirle otra carta de Ronda.   Siempre
pienso en mis amigos de los Estados Unidos.

Su afmo. amigo
Luis

B

I. *Cuestionario*

1. ¿ A dónde llegó Luis ?   2. ¿ A qué hora salió de
Algeciras ?   3. ¿ Quiénes eran los otros pasajeros ?   ¿ De
dónde eran ?   4. ¿ Por qué bajó Luis en cierta estación ?
5. ¿ Qué gritó un empleado ?   6. ¿ Quién acababa de
entrar en el compartimiento ?   7. ¿ Por qué tuvo miedo
Luis de no poder sentarse ?   8. ¿ Para quién eran los
paquetes ?   9. ¿ Dónde estaba el hijo del viejo ?
10. ¿ Eran ricos el viejo y su hijo ?

RONDA

II. *Temas*

1. La salida del tren.
2. Las cosas interesantes que vió Luis.
3. Los otros dos pasajeros del compartimiento.
4. El agua que compró Luis.
5. El viejo con muchos paquetes que subió al tren.
6. El hijo del viejo, y por qué estaba en Ronda.
7. El viejo y su hijo al llegar el tren a Ronda.
8. Lo que hizo Luis al llegar a Ronda.

C

JOHN. — Well, Louis, we are again seated in the train. Are you satisfied now? I like Europe greatly, especially Spain. I am not rich or I would be traveling all the time. I haven't any [1] silver mine in Peru. We shall have to look for a hotel with moderate prices at Granada, the 5 capital of this province. . . What time is it? . . . You have a beautiful watch. Is it gold?

LOUIS. — Yes, it is gold. It used to be my father's. It is now two o'clock. . . I am going [2] to say to the conductor that we are students, that we are Americans who have 10 just arrived from the United States, and that we are trying to learn Spanish. He will tell us where there is a comfortable hotel. He will be here soon. Where is he now? Is he in another car?

JOHN. — I haven't seen such a person on the train. You 15 will have to give the tickets to an employee near the exit in the depot. . . But why are you opening the window? Your hands are cold. What is the matter with you? Are you ill? You ought to be careful of your [3] health. You have just drunk two glasses of water. The water was cold but 20 it was not good. I believe that it is [4] from the river.

---

[1] ninguna (§ 36, 1).
[2] Ir requires a before infinitive (§ 166).
[3] la.
[4] Indicative.

LOUIS. — I am a little tired and I am hungry. I must eat something. When I was seasick on the boat, my uncle told me that eating was a good remedy. He is a doctor, — he is a good doctor, too.

5 JOHN. — What an enormous appetite! You have just eaten, and you feel like eating [1] again. Certainly your uncle, the doctor, would be satisfied with [2] you.

D

Drill

1. George V., the king of England, is ill.   2. I am a student, I am now in England but I am a South American. 3. I am from Peru and I am eighteen years old.   4. I am trying to learn English, French, and Italian.   5. I have to go now; I am ill.   6. On Tuesday, I must go to the office of Dr. Johnson, the best doctor in [3] this city. 7. He is an Englishman, and is now in the hotel near the depot.   8. We have just eaten some pears, some cherries, and other things.   9. What time is it? It will soon be four o'clock.   10. This watch is gold; it was my uncle's. 11. We have traveled one thousand, one hundred and ten kilometers.   12. Is it possible? What an interesting trip! 13. Two Englishmen were seated near the window. 14. They had the window open.   15. They were in Granada yesterday.   16. I should be very glad to go. 17. I doubt that they are (*pres. subj.*) here.   18. They will be in the library.   19. Are they Mexicans or Cubans? 20. He doubts that they are (*pres. subj.*) poor.

---

[1] Infinitive (§ **161**).   [2] de (§ **133**, footnote 3).
[3] de (§ **82**, footnote 4).

EXERCISE III

Plural of Nouns — Inflection, Agreement, and Position of Adjectives

20. Plural of nouns.[1] — 1. Nouns ending in unstressed vowels add -s.

Casa (*house*) — **casas** (*houses*); **cuarto** (*room*) — **cuartos** (*rooms*).

2. Nouns ending in consonants, and in **y**, commonly add -es.

Vapor (*steamer*) — **vapores** (*steamers*); **ley** (*law*) — **leyes** (*laws*).

(*a*) Final **z** becomes **c**, and final **c** becomes **qu**[2] in forming the plural.

Vez (*time*) — **veces** (*times*); **frac** (*dress coat*) — **fraques** (*dress coats*).

(*b*) Nouns ending in unstressed -es and -is, also compounds in -s, do not change.

Jueves (*Thursday*) — **jueves** (*Thursdays*); **sinopsis** (*synopsis*) — sinopsis (*synopses*); **paraguas** (*umbrella*) — **paraguas** (*umbrellas*).

21. Plural of adjectives. — Adjectives form their plural the same as nouns.

Bueno — **buenos**, *good;* **fácil** — **fáciles**, *easy;* **andaluz** — **andaluces**, *Andalusian.*

22. Feminine of adjectives. — 1. Adjectives which end in -o in the masculine singular change -o to -a to form the feminine.

Bueno — **buena**, *good;* **blanco** — **blanca**, *white.*

---

[1] The plural of certain masculine nouns may include both genders. **Los hermanos**, *the brothers*, or *the brother(s) and sister(s);* **los padres**, *the fathers* or *the parents;* **los reyes**, *the kings* or *the king(s) and queen(s).*

[2] This consonantal change is made to preserve the sound.

2. Adjectives which do not end in **-o** in the masculine (i.e., those which end in **-e** or a consonant) remain unchanged in the feminine.

> **Fuerte — fuerte,** *strong;* **azul — azul,** *blue.*

(*a*) Adjectives of nationality which end in a consonant, and other adjectives which end in **-án, -ón,** and **-or** (not comparative), add **-a** to the masculine to form the feminine.

Español — española, *Spanish;* **holgazán** [1] **— holgazana,** *lazy;* **preguntón** [1] **— preguntona,** *inquisitive;* **hablador — habladora,** *talkative.* But: **mejor** *m.* **— mejor** *f., better.*

23. Adjectives, and participles used adjectively, agree in gender and number with the nouns to which they refer.

Los cuadros hermosos.	The beautiful pictures.
Los libros escritos en español.	The books written in Spanish.
Las casas son pequeñas.	The houses are small.

24. Position of adjectives. — There is considerable freedom in the sentence position of adjectives. A descriptive adjective follows its noun, if it distinguishes one object from others of its kind; it precedes, if it denotes an inherent quality.

1. *After their nouns.* [2] — Adjectives of nationality, long adjectives, adjectives modified by adverbs, and past participles used as adjectives most commonly follow their nouns. [3]

Las frutas cubanas.	The Cuban fruits.
Un niño holgazán.	A lazy child.
Un hombre muy fuerte.	A very strong man.
Una ventana abierta.	An open window.

2. *Before or after their nouns.* — Certain adjectives may precede or follow their nouns. They follow when they

---

[1] For the treatment of the written accent, see Appendix A.

[2] If two or more adjectives follow a noun, **y,** *and,* is placed between the final two. **Una lección larga y difícil,** *a long, difficult lesson.*

[3] For the sentence position of superlative forms, see **§ 82,** footnote 2.

have their literal meaning; they precede when they express inherent qualities or are used in a figurative sense.

AFTER	BEFORE
El niño pobre, *the poor* (not rich) *child.*	El pobre niño, *the poor* (to be pitied) *child.*
Un hombre grande, *a large man.*	Un gran hombre, *a great man.*
La casa blanca, *the white house.*	La blanca nieve, *the white snow.*
Una noticia cierta, *a reliable piece of news.*	Cierta ciudad, *a certain city.*

25. Apocopation of adjectives.[1] — The following adjectives drop their final -o when they precede a masculine noun or adjective in the singular: **bueno, malo, uno, alguno, ninguno, primero, tercero,** and **postrero.**

El **buen** muchacho, *the good boy;* **algún** día, *some day;* **ningún** otro lápiz, *no other pencil.*

26. Adjectives are often used as nouns: —

El **cojo,** *the lame man;* la **joven,** *the young woman;* los **pobres,** *the poor people;* el **grande** y el **pequeño,** *the large one* [2] *and the small one* [2]; lo **bueno** y lo **malo,** *good and evil.*

VERBS

27. **Hacer,** *to make, do*

PRES. PART. haciendo; PAST PART. hecho.
PRES. IND. **hago,** haces, hace, hacemos, hacéis, hacen.
PRES. SUBJ. **haga, hagas, haga, hagamos, hagáis, hagan.**

---

[1] (a) **Grande** usually becomes **gran** before a singular noun of either gender, the full form **grande** being occasionally retained for oratorical effect. **El gran capitán,** *the great captain.* BUT: **Una grande desgracia,** *a great misfortune.* (b) **Santo** becomes **San** before a masculine name, unless the name begins with **To** or **Do: San Juan; San Antonio; San Francisco.** BUT: **Santo Domingo.** (c) **Ciento** becomes **cien** before the noun it modifies, even if an adjective intervenes. However **ciento** is used in numerals above *one hundred.* **Cien buenos automóviles,** *one hundred good automobiles.* BUT: **Ciento quince estudiantes,** *one hundred and fifteen students.*

[2] The English word *one* in the above use is not expressed in Spanish.

IMPF. IND. hacía, etc.; FUT. IND. haré, etc.; COND. haría, etc.
PRET. IND. hice, hiciste, hizo, hicimos, hicisteis, hicieron.
IMPF. SUBJS. hiciese, etc.; hiciera, etc.; FUT. SUBJ. hiciere, etc.
IMPERATIVES haz, haced.

28.   Decir, *to say*

PRES. PART. diciendo; PAST PART. dicho.
PRES. IND. digo, dices, dice, decimos, decís, dicen.
PRES. SUBJ. diga, digas, diga, digamos, digáis, digan.
IMPF. IND. decía, etc.; FUT. IND. diré, etc.; COND. diría, etc.
PRET. IND. dije, dijiste, dijo, dijimos, dijisteis, dijeron.
IMPF. SUBJS. dijese, etc.; dijera, etc.; FUT. SUBJ. dijere, etc.
IMPERATIVES di, decid.

IDIOMS

29.
$$\left.\begin{array}{l} \left\{\begin{array}{l} \textit{Haga Vd. el favor de } (\,+\textit{infinitive})\\ \textit{Hagan Vds.} \end{array}\right. \\[4pt] \left\{\begin{array}{l} \textit{Tenga Vd. la bondad de } (\,+\textit{infinitive})\\ \textit{Tengan Vds.} \end{array}\right. \\[4pt] \left\{\begin{array}{l} \textit{Sírvase Vd. } (\,+\textit{infinitive})\\ \textit{Sírvanse Vds.} \end{array}\right. \end{array}\right\} \text{Please}$$

Haga Vd. el favor de *or* Tenga   Please open the door.
Vd. la bondad de *or* Sírvase Vd.
abrir la puerta.

30. *Hacer* (*+ period of time*)   (*Period of time*) ago
Hace ocho días.   A week ago.

(*Invisible phenomena*)

31. *Hacer calor,* to be warm   *Hacer viento,* to be windy
    Hacer frío, to be cold   *Hacer buen* (*mal*) *tiempo,*
                                          to be good (bad) weather

Hace frío, it is cold.   Hacía viento, it was windy.

(*Visible phenomena*)

32. *Haber polvo,* to be dusty   *Haber luna,* to be moonlight

Hay polvo, it is dusty.   Habrá luna, it will be moonlight.

(Hacer *or* haber)

33. *Hacer or haber sol*   To be sunny, the sun is
                                  shining

Hacía (había) sol.   It was sunny (The sun was
                                  shining).

A

Ronda, 24 de junio de 19—.

Querido amigo:

Me acuerdo de haberle dicho a Vd. que le escribiría
muchas veces durante los meses del verano. Como Vd.
ve, lo hago, pues ya he escrito dos veces antes de hoy.
También estoy seguro de que ningún otro amigo le diría tan 5
fielmente lo que ve.

Ayer, como hacía buen tiempo, tuve ganas de aprender
un poco acerca de la vida de los campesinos andaluces.
Para llegar al campo tuve que pasar por el Puente Nuevo
sobre el Guadelevín, río de importancia cerca de la ciudad. 10
Al pasar por el puente vi las huertas y las casitas de los
campesinos a unos cincuenta metros más abajo en el valle.
Hacía viento, y un pobre cojo estaba pidiendo limosna,
sentado al borde del camino, donde había mucho polvo.
Le pregunté si sabía un buen camino para bajar al valle. 15
Una niña pobre y haraposa que estaba con él me dijo que,
aunque no había camino verdadero, me enseñaría un buen
sendero por donde bajaban los campesinos con sus burros.
Di al cojo una limosnita, y la niña me condujo a una casa
blanca, que no estaba muy lejos, desde donde me mostró 20
el sendero deseado.

Caminé por el sendero, y al fin llegué a una huerta bien
labrada con buenas legumbres y con unos árboles frutales.
En aquel momento llegó otro hombre con unos libros en la
mano. Me dijo que era maestro, y que venía dos veces por 25
semana al valle, en donde iba de casa en casa. Los campesinos no tenían otra escuela. Un niño que estaba regando

los cuadros fértiles de la huerta corrió a su casa de donde
salió su padre a recibirnos. — Tengan la bondad de entrar
en la casa — nos dijo. Lo hicimos, y el maestro se sentó
en una silla grande cerca de una mesita redonda. Dió al
5 niño lecciones de lectura y de aritmética. Los padres
parecían muy ufanos de los conocimientos del discípulo.
Les dije adiós, y me fuí a visitar los molinos de harina del
valle. Vi muchas otras cosas interesantes, pero no tengo
tiempo para contarlas hoy.
10   Espero escribir la próxima vez desde Sevilla.

Con muchos recuerdos,

Luis

B

I. *Cuestionario*

1. ¿ Había escrito Luis a su amigo muchas veces?
2. ¿ Qué tiempo hacía cuando salió de Ronda?   3. ¿ Por
qué salió de la ciudad?   4. ¿ Qué vió Luis al pasar por
el puente?   5. ¿ Quién le enseñó un buen sendero para
bajar al valle?   6. ¿ Quiénes bajaban por ese sendero?
7. ¿ Qué hacía un niño en la huerta de su padre?
8. ¿ Quién llegó al mismo tiempo que Luis?   9. ¿ Qué
hizo el maestro?   10. ¿ Vió Luis otras cosas interesantes?

II. *Temas*

1. Luis tiene cuidado de es-   4. El sendero del valle.
   cribir a su amigo.   5. El niño de la huerta.
2. Luis sale de Ronda por   6. La llegada del maestro.
   el Puente Nuevo.   7. Las lecciones del niño.
3. El pobre cojo y la niña   8. Las otras cosas que vió
   haraposa.   Luis.

C

Louis (*to a traveler seated near the closed window*). — It is
very warm to-day, sir, and I am warm. Please open the

window. Many thanks. . . John, do you see [1] the poor
lame man? He is an old man, ragged and poor. And do
you see [1] the beautiful woman seated in that large automobile near the poor man? What a contrast! Andalusian
women are very pretty, lively and charming. I have seen [1] 5
many Spanish women who have eyes black as coal. Many
American girls have eyes blue as the sky.

JOHN. — Be [2] careful, Louis, you are not a poet, you [3]
are a student. . . Tell [2] me the contents of the large suitcase which you have just opened. . . Please write in Spanish 10
the names of all the things. — It is more interesting to [4]
study Spanish in Spain or in South America than in Professor Álvarez' class. Many American students, who are
talkative and lazy when they are studying Spanish in the
United States, try to learn quickly in Spain. 15

LOUIS. — Very well. Here is the list, — a Spanish fan;
a history of Spain, written in English; some red and white
pencils; an English penknife; a package of very large
pins; some French postcards; a round mirror; a blue
necktie; a dozen [5] linen handkerchiefs. . . Whew, it is hot 20
in this train! That is enough; my eyes are tired.

JOHN. — Poor man! Haven't you a headache, too?
The sun is not shining now and soon it will be cooler. . .
You said, ten minutes ago, that you had a history of Spain,
written in English. I have one written in Spanish. Unfor- 25
tunately, some careless child has torn out the first chapter,
the third map, and some other pages. What a pity!

D

Drill

1. Mr. Pérez, please close the large windows. 2. We
shall be cold. 3. The weather is bad to-day, but it will

---

[1] Use **a** with personal dir. obj. (§ **38**).

[2] Pres. subj. used as imperative, (§ **52**).

[3] Omit (§ **72**).   [4] No preposition (§ **163**).   [5] Insert **de.**

be good weather to-morrow.   4. Professor Álvarez says
that American girls are not lazy nor talkative.   5. They
keep studying all the time.   6. Some have black eyes,
others have blue eyes.   7. They have just read *Captain
Veneno*, a story of a great captain.   8. Was he a large
man?   9. John said, two days ago, that he had many
brothers and sisters.   10. The names of the saints, Saint
Francis and Saint Anthony, were given [1] to certain cities
in the United States.   11. I shall tell other interesting
things to-morrow.   12. I want you to tell (*pres. subj.*)
me the names of the white objects on the table.   13. It
is often dusty in summer in Madrid because it is very
sunny.   14. The water is cold but it is not good.   15. Do
we have to study, on Tuesday, the third chapter of the
first volume?   16. I doubt that it will be (*pres. subj.*)
cold to-morrow.   17. They made the bridge a year ago.
18. Do the work soon.   19. Tell me the truth.   20. George
Washington, the first president of the United States, always
told [2] the truth.

EXERCISE IV

Gender of Nouns — Negation — Interrogation — Direct Object with *a*

34. Masculine gender: [3] — 1. Names of male beings,
days, months, rivers, oceans, mountains, and infinitives
used as nouns.

El hombre, *the man;* el lunes, *Monday;* febrero, *February;* el
Amazonas, *the Amazon;* el Atlántico, *the Atlantic;* los Andes, *the
Andes;* el hablar, *speaking.*

---

[1] se dieron a (§ **131,** 4).   [2] Imperfect indicative (§ **47**).
[3] Some nouns have two genders with different meanings:

el capital, *the capital* (money)	la capital, *the capital* (city)
el guía, *the guide* (man)	la guía, *the guide* (book)
el parte, *the message*	la parte, *the part*

2. Nouns ending in -o, and many nouns ending in -l, -r, and -ma.[1]

El libro, *the book;* el ángel, *the angel;* el azúcar, *the sugar;* el idioma, *the language.*

35. Feminine gender:[1] — 1. Names of female beings, letters of the alphabet, and most cities.

La mujer, *the woman;* la j (jota), *j;* la Habana, *Havana.*

2. Nouns ending in -a, -ión, -d, -umbre, and -ie.[2]

La mesa, *the table;* la canción, *the song;* la ciudad, *the city;* la costumbre, *the custom;* la serie, *the series.*

36. Negation. — Negation is usually expressed by no placed before the verb (before the auxiliary in compound tenses). Nothing but object pronouns may intervene between no and the verb.

No tienen jardines.	They do not have gardens.
No han venido.	They have not come.
No los hemos visto.	We have not seen them.

1. Certain negative words, ninguno,[3] nada, nadie, nunca, jamás, ni and tampoco require no before the verb when they follow it;[4] when they precede the verb (*for emphasis*) or when they stand alone, no is not used.

No viene ninguno de mis amigos.	None of my friends is coming.
No ha dicho nada.	He has not said anything.

---

[1] Common exceptions: la mano, *the hand;* la sal, *the salt;* la col, *the cabbage;* la miel, *the honey;* la catedral, *the cathedral;* la flor, *the flower;* la pluma, *the pen;* la plataforma, *the platform.*

[2] Common exceptions: el día, *the day;* el mapa, *the map;* many nouns in ma; el gorrión, *the sparrow;* el sarampión, *the measles;* el sud, *the south;* el pie, *the foot.*

[3] Alguno may be used with negative value, if no precedes the verb. No tuvo cosa alguna, *he had nothing.* Alguién and algo (opposites of nadie and nada) may not be used negatively.

[4] In contrast to English and French, no negative word may come between the auxiliary and the past participle in Spanish. See § 4, 1, footnote 4. No le he visto nunca, *I have never seen him.*

Nadie irá.	Nobody will go.
Nunca (jamás) le veré.	Never shall I see him.
Ni él tampoco vendrá.	Nor will he come either.

2. *But*, as a conjunction, is most commonly **pero** (occasionally **mas**). *But*, after a negative verb, is **sino**, when no verb follows, or when the following verb is in the infinitive.[1]

Escribe el español, pero no lo habla.	He writes Spanish, but he does not speak it.
No voy a París, sino a Madrid.	I am not going to Paris, but to Madrid.
Juan no quiere jugar, sino estudiar.	John does not want to play, but to study.

(*a*) The word *only* (*nothing but*) may be expressed by **no . . . sino** or **no . . . más que.**[2]

No bebemos sino (más que) agua.	We drink only (nothing but) water.

37. Interrogative sentence order. [3]— In interrogative, as in declarative sentences, the word order is quite flexible in Spanish. A common order in questions is (1) verb, (2) noun object or predicate adjective, (3) subject. However, if the noun object with its modifiers is longer than the subject, the subject precedes.[4]

¿ Es buena el agua ?	Is the water good ?
¿ Tiene agua Carlos ?	Does Charles have any water ?
¿ Tiene Carlos agua muy fría ?	Does Charles have very cold water ?

---

[1] *But* is usually **sino que,** when the first verb is negative, and the second, in contrast, is different, and affirmative, and not in the infinitive. **Luis no estudia, sino que juega,** *Louis is not studying, but* (*on the contrary*) *he is playing.*

[2] *Only* may also be expressed by **sólo** or **solamente. Bebemos sólo (solamente) agua,** *We drink only water.*

[3] An inverted interrogation point must be placed at the beginning of a question.

[4] For the sentence position of pronoun objects, see § **74.**

La Torre del Oro y la Catedral con la Giralda, Sevilla

S<small>ALA DE LOS</small> E<small>MBAJADORES EN EL GRAN</small> A<small>LCÁZAR DE</small> S<small>EVILLA</small>

38. Direct object with *a*.[1] — The preposition **a** (*not to be translated*) is used before the direct object, when the direct object is: (1) a definite personal noun, (2) a geographical proper name, and (3) a pronoun (except a conjunctive pronoun and the relative **que**) referring to a person.[2]

Buscábamos a Carlos.	We were looking for Charles.
Visitaremos a Madrid.	We shall visit Madrid.
No he visto a nadie.	I have not seen anybody.

VERBS

39. Querer, *to wish*

Pres. Part. queriendo; Past Part. querido.

Pres. Ind. quiero, quieres, quiere, queremos, queréis, quieren.

Pres. Subj. quiera, quieras, quiera, queramos, queráis, quieran.

Impf. Ind. quería, etc.; Fut. Ind. querré, etc.; Cond. querría, etc.

Pret. Ind. quise, quisiste, quiso, quisimos, quisisteis, quisieron.

Impf. Subjs. quisiese, etc.; quisiera, etc.; Fut. Subj. quisiere, etc.

Imperatives quiere, quered.

40. Poner, *to put*

Pres. Part. poniendo; Past Part. puesto.

Pres. Ind. pongo, pones, pone, ponemos, ponéis, ponen.

Pres. Subj. ponga, pongas, ponga, pongamos, pongáis, pongan.

Impf. Ind. ponía, etc.; Fut. Ind. pondré, etc.; Cond. pondría, etc.

Pret. Ind. puse, pusiste, puso, pusimos, pusisteis, pusieron.

Impf. Subjs. pusiese, etc.; pusiera, etc.; Fut. Subj. pusiere, etc.

Imperatives pon, poned.

---

[1] When the verb has a direct (personal) object and an indirect object, the direct object does not take **a**. **Envió su hijo al correo,** *He sent his son to the post office.*

[2] With nouns not designated in the above list **a** may be used to avoid doubt as to the direct object. **Ve el toro al caballo,** *The bull sees the horse.* **Ve al toro el caballo,** *The horse sees the bull.*

IDIOMS

41. *Querer decir*	To mean
¿ Qué quiere decir eso?	What does that mean?
42. *A menudo*	Often
Viene a verme a menudo.	He often comes to see me.
43. *Gustar a* (*uno*)	To please (one), like
Me gusta el sombrero.	I like the hat (the hat pleases me).

A

Sevilla, 6 de julio de 19—.

Querido amigo:

Me gusta mucho esta ciudad famosa. Me ofrece tantas cosas interesantes que temo no acabar nunca con mi carta, si digo todo lo que quiero. La torre alta de la Giralda, el
5 gran Alcázar, y las calles estrechas y tortuosas de esta ciudad andaluza recuerdan la edad mora, edad romántica y de gran interés histórico. La vida íntima de familia tiene su centro en el patio de la casa. Por la noche hay tertulias en los patios. Me gustan las fuentes, las flores y las palmas
10 que dan un encanto singular a tal escena. A los andaluces les gusta la música, y a menudo al pasearme de noche por las calles, oigo de casi todas las puertas abiertas canciones alegres acompañadas del sonido de las guitarras. ¡ Qué vida tan encantadora !
15 Anteayer fué el 4 de julio. Cuando me levanté, me dije: « ¿ Qué haré para celebrar nuestro día de independencia? ¿ No hay nada que hacer aquí en Sevilla? ¿ No vendrá tampoco ningún conocido español para felicitarme en este día? No, nadie querrá venir. ¿ Podría yo encontrar
20 algo de América en Sevilla? Pues sí, los españoles han puesto en la catedral el sarcófago del gran descubridor de América, Cristóbal Colón. » Fuí a pasar un rato en la catedral. ¿ Ha oído Vd. alguna vez el dicho: « A Castilla

y a León nuevo mundo dió Colón? » Este dicho es muy conocido en España.

Ya hace más de cuatro siglos que los descubridores españoles atravesaron el Atlántico, descubrieron el Amazonas y el Pacífico, y aun penetraron en los Andes. Cambiaron el mapa del mundo conocido. Para saber más de la historia de los descubridores de las Américas subí a la biblioteca colombina, que contiene más de treinta mil tomos. Pasé dos horas mirando los libros viejos, sobre todo los de Cristóbal Colón con apuntes marginales en su propia letra. No hay modo más interesante de celebrar nuestro día nacional en esta parte de Europa.

Tenga la bondad de dar mis recuerdos más sinceros a todos mis amigos.   Su afmo.

Luis

B

I. *Cuestionario*

1. ¿Qué cosas recuerdan la edad mora de Sevilla?
2. ¿Para qué sirve el patio de la casa? 3. ¿Qué hay en un patio? 4. ¿Cuándo tienen música los sevillanos?
5. ¿Qué día de importancia llegó? 6. ¿Quisieron venir muchos amigos para felicitar a Luis? 7. ¿En dónde encontró Luis algo de interés para un americano? 8. ¿Qué dicho español hay acerca de Colón? 9. ¿Cuánto tiempo hace que atravesaron el Atlántico los primeros descubridores? 10. ¿Qué hay en la biblioteca colombina?

II. *Temas*

1. Las cosas de interés histórico en Sevilla.
2. El patio y su contenido.
3. Las tertulias.
4. Las dificultades para celebrar el 4 de julio en Sevilla.
5. La tumba de Cristóbal Colón.
6. Los descubridores españoles.
7. La biblioteca colombina y los libros viejos de Colón.

C

LOUIS. — I can never learn[1] to talk Spanish. Never
have I heard such a language. There is nothing more
disagreeable. Have you ever seen a more difficult language?
None of my Spanish friends speak slowly enough. No one
5 speaks slowly. And Mr. Díaz, our guide with the large
hat, is no good. He knows nothing of the map of Spain. . .
It is often bad weather, too. It is hot and windy and very
dusty. I do not like Spain.

JOHN. — What do you mean? It will be good weather
10 to-morrow. And the Spanish language is not hard. When
you do not understand a Spaniard, why do you not say,
" Please speak more slowly. What do those[2] words mean,
sir ? " You are right concerning our guide. Mr. Díaz
does not know much about the south of Spain. He is
15 from Saint Sebastian, a city of northern Spain, and is
well acquainted only with the part of Spain near the
Pyrenees. But you have only to buy a good Spanish
guide-book. . . I am well satisfied here in Spain. I do
not speak Spanish well. On the other hand, I am be-
20 ginning to read the language easily. I like the Spanish
language and also the songs and all the customs. What
is the matter with you? I have never seen anybody so
gloomy.

LOUIS. — I am not well this morning. I have eaten
25 nothing, and I drank only hot water. I am not homesick,
but I should be very glad to cross the Atlantic like
Christopher Columbus, and see once more my old friend
(ƒ.), the Statue of Liberty.

---

[1] Note that verbs of *learning, teaching, beginning,* and verbs of *motion*
regularly require the preposition **a** before an infinitive (§ **166**).

[2] **esas** (§ **108**).

D

Drill

1. Waiter, put the coffee and the sugar on the round table. 2. The coffee will soon be cold. 3. I shall put nothing on the round table, — never. 4. No one puts anything on it. 5. I put a few songs and the guide-book on it, a week ago, and it broke.[1] 6. The table is beautiful, but it is not strong. 7. Do you wish a cup of coffee, Mrs. Martin? 8. I drink only chocolate. 9. Would you like some [2] chocolate, Captain Martin? 10. A thousand thanks, but I drink only cold water. 11. No chocolate is good. 12. Never have I drunk good chocolate. 13. Nor I, either. 14. I have never wanted anything but water. 15. On the other hand, I am often hungry. 16. What do you mean? 17. Have they put the money on the table? 18. They said that they would do it. 19. They did not wish (*pret.*) to do it. 20. It was cold yesterday, but it will be warm to-morrow. 21. It will be sunny but it will also be dusty. 22. Please write an " H " on the blackboard.

---

[1] se quebró (§ 131, 3).   [2] Omit.

EXERCISE V

Tenses of the Indicative Mood — Imperative

44. Present, future, and conditional. — The present [1] and future tenses in Spanish are usually employed as in English. The conditional (*past future*) in Spanish is expressed in English by *should* [2] or *would* [2] followed by the infinitive.[3]

Juan compra recuerdos.	John buys (is buying) souvenirs.
Comprará un automóvil.	He will buy an automobile.
Dijo que compraría una casa.	He said that he would buy a house.

45. The future tense may express a probable present state or action, and the conditional (*past future*) a probable past one.

¿Qué hora es? — Serán las dos.	What time is it? It is probably (possibly) two o'clock, *or*, It must be two o'clock.
¿Qué hora era? — Serían las once.	What time was it? It was probably (possibly) eleven o'clock, *or*, It must have been eleven o'clock.

46. Action or state which began in the past and is still continuing in the present, indicated in English by the present perfect, is expressed in Spanish by the present tense with **hace . . . que.**

Hace diez días que estoy aquí.	I have been here for ten days.

---

[1] For the progressive construction, see §§ **14**, 3 and **169**.

[2] The words *will* and *would*, when they mean *to wish* or *to be willing*, are expressed in Spanish by forms of **querer**. The word *should*, when it means *ought*, is expressed in Spanish by forms of **deber**.

¿Quiere Vd. darme cinco pesetas?	Will you (are you willing to) give me five pesetas?
¿Querría Vd. ir conmigo mañana?	Would you go with me to-morrow?
Debemos hablar despacio.	We should (ought to) speak slowly.

[3] See uses of the imperfect (*past*) subjunctive, §§ **151**, **153**.

47. Imperfect. — The imperfect (*past descriptive*) tense is used to describe (1) continued or habitual past action or state, and (2) to express an action or state of affairs when something else happened.

Hablábamos español **cuando vivíamos en Méjico.**	We used to speak Spanish when we lived in Mexico.
Jugaban **cuando llegamos.**	They were playing when we arrived.

48. Action or state beginning in the past and continuing up to a certain stated time in the past, indicated in English by the pluperfect (*past perfect*), is expressed in Spanish by the imperfect (*past descriptive*) with **hacía . . . que.**

Hacía dos meses que estábamos en Sevilla cuando llegó.
We had been in Seville two months when he arrived.

49. Preterite. — The preterite (*past absolute*) tense expresses a completed definite past action or state.

Luisa vino ayer.	Louise came yesterday.
Estuvo enfermo dos meses.	He was ill two months.

50. Present Perfect. — The present perfect expresses (1) a past action not referring to any definite time; (2) a past action which still affects the present condition of affairs. Its use corresponds to that of the English present perfect.

He estado en España.	I have been in Spain.
Dice que han llegado.	He says that they have arrived.

51. Pluperfect. — The pluperfect (*past perfect*) in Spanish generally corresponds in use to the English pluperfect (*past perfect*). The past anterior (*second past perfect*) indicates an action that took place immediately before another past action. It follows such conjunctions of time as **así que, luego que, tan pronto como,** *as soon as,* **apenas,** *hardly,* etc.

Habían vivido en Barcelona.	They had lived in Barcelona.
Luego que hubieron llegado a Segovia, buscaron sus baúles.	As soon as they had reached Segovia they looked for their trunks.

52. Imperative. — 1. In familiar speech [1] the distinctively imperative forms are used in affirmative commands; in negative commands, the present subjunctive (*second person sing. and pl.*) must be used.

Habla (*sing.*), **hablad** (*pl.*).	Speak.
No hables (*sing.*), **no habléis** (*pl.*).	Do not speak.

2. In formal speech,[1] both affirmative and negative commands are expressed by the present subjunctive (*third person sing. and pl.*) with **usted** and **ustedes**.

Hable Vd. (*sing.*), **hablen Vds.** (*pl.*).	Speak.
No hable Vd. (*sing.*), **no hablen Vds.** (*pl.*).	Do not speak.

VERBS

53.   **Ir,** *to go*

Pres. Part. **yendo**; Past Part. **ido.**
Pres. Ind. **voy, vas, va, vamos, vais, van.**
Pres. Subj. **vaya, vayas, vaya, vayamos, vayáis, vayan.**
Impf. Ind. **iba, ibas, iba, íbamos, ibais, iban.**
Fut. Ind. **iré,** etc.; Cond. **iría,** etc.
Pret. Ind. **fuí, fuiste, fué, fuimos, fuisteis, fueron.**
Impf. Subjs. **fuese,** etc.; **fuera,** etc.; Fut. Subj. **fuere,** etc.
Imperatives **ve, vamos,** id.

54.   **Andar,** *to go*

(*With no idea of definite destination or purpose.*)

Pres. Part. **andando**; Past Part. **andado.**
Pres. Ind. **ando, andas, anda, andamos, andáis, andan.**
Pres. Subj. **ande, andes, ande, andemos, andéis, anden.**
Impf. Ind. **andaba,** etc.; Fut. Ind. **andaré,** etc.; Cond. **andaría,** etc.
Pret. Ind. **anduve, anduviste, anduvo, anduvimos, anduvisteis, anduvieron.**
Impf. Subjs. **anduviese,** etc.; **anduviera,** etc.; Fut. Subj. **anduviere,** etc.
Imperatives **anda, andad.**

---

[1] See § **73.**

IDIOMS

55. *Poco a poco*   Little by little, gently

Vamos aprendiendo poco a poco.   We are learning little by little.

56. *A la vez*   At the same time

Trabajan y hablan a la vez.   They work and talk at the same time.

57. *Al menos*
    A lo menos ⎬ At least
    Por lo menos

Hemos hecho al menos (a lo menos) (por lo menos) lo más necesario.

We have done at least what is most necessary.

A

Córdoba, 8 de julio de 19—.

Querido Alberto:

Hace más de tres semanas que estoy en España, y poco a poco aprendo a hablar bien el español. Al menos comprendo casi todo lo que me dicen los españoles, pero no sé siempre las mejores palabras para expresar lo que 5 quiero decir. Me acuerdo de que ya hacía muchos meses que estudiaba el español, cuando nos dijo nuestro profesor: « Si hablan Vds. un idioma extranjero, y no saben las palabras deseadas, es mejor rodear la montaña que subirla. » — Quería decir que no sería bueno tratar de buscar cierta 10 palabra desconocida, sino que debíamos emplear otra que no fuera muy diferente. Era buen consejo y muy útil.

Esta tarde hacía mucho calor, y yo no quería andar por las calles. Serían las cinco cuando fuí a un café. Otro joven, que parecía extranjero, estaba sentado a una mesa, 15 y me senté cerca de él. Estaba leyendo un periódico y fumando a la vez. Llamé a un mozo, porque tenía mucha sed. — ¿ Qué quiere Vd. tomar, caballero ? — ¿ Qué hay

que beber hoy? Quiero decir, ¿ qué bebida fría hay? —
Hay cerveza alemana, un buen vino de Rioja, y agua con
azucarillos. — ¡ Caramba ! no los deseo. Daría un mundo
por un . . . « ice cream ». No sé cómo se llama en español.
5 ¿ Será una crema congelada ? No hay tal cosa en España,
supongo. — El mozo pareció no comprender.

El joven que leía el periódico, lo puso en la mesa, y dijo:
— Sí, señor, tendrán lo que desea Vd. Mozo, ¿ no tienen
Vds. helados ? — Pues sí, señor, hoy tenemos helados de
10 fresa y de cereza. — ¿ Es posible ? grité. ¡ Qué sorpresa !
Caballero, le agradezco muchísimo. Tenga la bondad de
tomar un helado conmigo. — Con mucho gusto. — Mozo,
tráiganos dos helados de cereza. — Sí, señor. — Caballero,
¿ es Vd. norteamericano ? — No, señor, soy inglés, pero he
15 vivido en Filadelfia.

Hablábamos de la vida americana cuando el mozo
volvió con los helados. Estaban deliciosos. Tomaré helados
a menudo. Al fin pagué al mozo la cuenta, y salimos del
café. Nos habíamos divertido, y yo había aprendido una
20 palabra muy útil « helado ». En esta carta no le he dicho
nada de las maravillas de Córdoba, ni una palabra de
la famosa mezquita árabe a donde van todos los turistas.
¡ Qué lástima ! Algún día le veré, y se lo diré todo.

Hasta otra vez,

Luis

B

I. *Cuestionario*

1. ¿ Cuántas semanas hace que Luis está en España ?
2. ¿ Comprende y habla bien el español ?   3. ¿ Qué había
dicho el profesor ?   4. ¿ Por qué no quería Luis andar
por las calles ?   5. ¿ Quién leía un periódico en el café ?
6. ¿ Qué bebidas tenían en el café ?   7. ¿ Qué quería
tomar Luis ?   8. ¿ Qué clase de helados tomaron Luis y
el inglés ?   9. ¿ Dónde había vivido el inglés ?   10. ¿ Des-
cribió Luis en su carta la mezquita de Córdoba ?

II. *Temas*

1. Luis aprende a hablar bien el español.
2. El profesor de Luis y sus consejos.
3. El joven extranjero en el café.
4. Las bebidas del café.
5. Las dificultades de Luis.
6. El joven extranjero ayuda a Luis.
7. Los dos helados de cereza.
8. El país del extranjero.
9. Las maravillas de Córdoba.

C

Louis. — Where [1] did you go, John? I have been looking for you a long time. Why do you go thus through the streets? You never buy anything.

John. — It was hot, and I was looking for a good café. I found a little one [2] where it was cool. I was eating [3] a 5 strawberry ice-cream, and at the same time was talking with the waiter when you entered.

Louis. — Listen, John, I have just received a postcard from Mary Anderson who went to school with me [4] a few years ago. For several months she has been traveling in 10 France and [5] England with her mother, in an [2] automobile. They are now in Spain, and [5] will go soon to Granada.

John. — I have never seen Miss Anderson, nor her mother, either. Are they possibly in Seville to-day? Does Miss Anderson speak Spanish? Is she pretty? 15

Louis. — Oh, come now! Do not ask so many questions. They are probably somewhere in this province. Mary, at least, tries to speak Spanish, and she will learn it soon. She used to be very talkative.

John. — I do not like American girls very [6] much. But, 20

---

[1] **A dónde.**   [2] Omit.   [3] **tomar.**
[4] **conmigo** (§ **71**, footnote 3).
[5] **e** is used instead of **y** before words beginning with **i** or **hi.**
[6] Omit *very.*

tell me, Louis, how old is she? Are her eyes blue or black?
Why did she make this trip?

Louis. — It is very clear that you do not like American
girls. "Better late than never." She left New York
5 three months ago. For several years she had wanted to go
to Europe. She talked often of the trip and kept saving
money little by little. As soon as she had obtained a part
of the sum desired she went to see her uncle. He had
promised to help her. He did what[1] he had promised,
10 and she is here. She is young and pretty. Would you
like to make her acquaintance?

D

Drill

1. We were talking to the girls when the professor
entered. 2. What did he say? What did he do? 3. He
said nothing; he will never tell us. 4. He went soon.
5. It is probably ten o'clock. 6. It was probably nine
o'clock yesterday when you entered[2] the café. 7. He
was never a teacher of Spanish. 8. I have been learning
the language, little by little, for two years. 9. We went
to Europe, a year ago. 10. I told my father that I would
go to church.[3] 11. We used to go often to the theaters.
12. They said that they would go to the south of Spain
next year. 13. They will work and talk at the same
time. 14. Are you ever going to study Portuguese?
15. I have never gone to France. 16. Nor I, either.
17. At least, I want him to go (*pres. subj.*) to South America.
18. Let us go home;[4] I have to study. 19. Be careful;
do not put your[5] feet on the chair. 20. He put the
chair near the door.

---

[1] lo que (§ **122,** 4).   [2] Use **en.**   [3] Use def. art.
         [4] **a casa.**   [5] **los** (§ **97**).

EXERCISE VI

Numbers — Seasons — Months — Days — Time — Money

58. Cardinal numbers. — The table of cardinal numbers is as follows:

0	cero	14	catorce	80	ochenta
1	uno,[1] una	15	quince	90	noventa
2	dos	16	diez y seis [2]	100	ciento [1]
3	tres	17	diez y siete	101	ciento uno
4	cuatro	18	diez y ocho	110	ciento diez
5	cinco	19	diez y nueve	116	ciento diez y seis
6	seis	20	veinte	200	doscientos, –as
7	siete	21	veinte y uno [2]	300	trescientos, –as
8	ocho	22	veinte y dos	400	cuatrocientos, –as
9	nueve	30	treinta	500	quinientos, –as
10	diez	40	cuarenta	600	seiscientos, –as
11	once	50	cincuenta	700	setecientos, –as
12	doce	60	sesenta	800	ochocientos, –as
13	trece	70	setenta	900	novecientos, –as

1,000 = mil [3]; 1,000,000 = un millón

59. Ordinal numbers through *tenth:* —

primero, first	**sexto,** sixth
segundo, second	**séptimo,** seventh
tercero, third	**octavo,** eighth
cuarto, fourth	**noveno (nono),** ninth
quinto, fifth	**décimo,** tenth

(*a*) The ordinal numbers vary in ending for gender and number like adjectives ending in -o.[4]

---

[1] For the apocopated forms **un, cien, primer** and **tercer,** see § **25** and **25,** footnote 1.

[2] The following forms may also be used: **dieciséis, diecisiete, dieciocho, diecinueve, veintiuno, veintidós,** etc. Such contracted forms are found rarely in the *thirties* and not at all in the higher *tens.*

[3] Counting by hundreds is not done above *nine hundred* in Spanish; beginning with *ten hundred,* **mil** is used. **Mil novecientos veinte y cinco,** *nineteen hundred and twenty-five.*

[4] §§ **21, 22,**1.

60. Use of ordinal numbers. — The use of ordinals is more limited in Spanish than in English.

1. Days of the month, except the *first*, are expressed by the cardinal numbers.[1]

El primero de mayo.	The first of May.
El dos de agosto.	The second of August.

2. With titles of sovereigns and popes, the ordinal numbers are used through *tenth;* after that, cardinal numbers are used.

Carlos quinto.	Charles Fifth.
Pío nono.	Pius Ninth.
Alfonso trece.	Alphonso Thirteenth.

3. With chapters, pages, volumes, paragraphs, etc., both cardinal and ordinal numbers are used through *ten;* above *ten*, only cardinals are commonly used.

La tercera página.	The third page.
Página tres.	Page three.
Página catorce.	Page fourteen.

61. Fractions through *tenth* have a cardinal number as numerator, and an ordinal as denominator; after *tenth*, the denominator is an ordinal in **-avo,** formed on the corresponding cardinal.

$\frac{3}{4}$=tres cuartos,[2] $\frac{5}{6}$=cinco sextos; $\frac{2}{13}$=dos trezavos.

(*a*) *Half* is expressed by **medio** as an adjective, and by **mitad** as a noun. *Third* is expressed by **tercio.**

Dos libras y media.	Two pounds and a half.
La mitad de la manzana.	One half of the apple.
Dos tercios de la página.	Two thirds of the page.

---

[1] The word *on* is not expressed in Spanish before the days of the week and the days of the month. **Vino el lunes,** *he came on Monday.* **Vino el ocho de julio,** *he came on the eighth of July.*

[2] The word **parte** may also be used to express fractional numbers: $\frac{3}{4}$ = **tres cuartas partes.**

62. Arithmetical signs: —

(+) **más** *or* **y**   (×) **(multiplicado) por** [1]   (=) **es, es igual a,**
(−) **menos**   (:) **dividido por**   **son, son**
                                                          iguales a

63. Seasons, months, days are rendered as follows: —

1. SEASONS: — **el invierno,** *winter;* **la primavera,** *spring;*
el verano, *summer;* **el otoño,** *autumn.*

2. MONTHS: — **enero,** *January;* **febrero,** *February;* **marzo,**
March; **abril,** *April;* **mayo,** *May;* **junio,** *June;* **julio,**
July; **agosto,** *August;* **septiembre,** *September;* **octubre,**
October; **noviembre,** *November;* **diciembre,** *December.*

3. DAYS: — **domingo,** *Sunday;* **lunes,** *Monday;* **martes,**
Tuesday; **miércoles,** *Wednesday;* **jueves,** *Thursday;* **viernes,**
Friday; **sábado,** *Saturday.*

64. Time of day. — The hour of day is expressed by the
cardinal number preceded by the feminine article and
followed by **y** or **menos** with the number of minutes or the
fraction of the hour.

¿ Qué hora es?	What time is it ?
Es la una y media.	It is half past one.
Son las tres y (un) cuarto.	It is a quarter past three.
Son las tres menos veinte.	It is twenty minutes to three.
Son las tres menos (un) cuarto.	It is a quarter to three.
Son las tres en punto.	It is exactly three o'clock.
¿ A qué hora?	At what time ?
A las siete de la mañana.[2]	At seven A.M.
A las dos de la tarde.[2]	At two P.M.
A las ocho de la noche.[2]	At eight P.M.

---

[1] **Veces,** *times,* is also used. **Tres veces nueve son veinte y siete,** *three*
times nine are twenty-seven. *Once* is expressed by **una vez,** *twice* by **dos**
veces.

[2] **Por la mañana, por la tarde,** and **por la noche** are used when the hour
of the day is not expressed. In some cases **en** may be found. **Iremos por**
la mañana (tarde, noche), *we shall go in the morning* (*afternoon, evening*).

65. Money. — In Spain the **peseta** is the monetary unit with a value of about *twenty cents*. 100 **céntimos** = 1 **peseta**. In many Spanish American countries the **peso** is the monetary unit. 100 **centavos** = 1 **peso**. The exchange rate varies according to the country concerned. The Mexican **peso** is worth about *fifty cents*.

VERBS

66.   Poder, *to be able, can*

PRES. PART. **pudiendo**; PAST PART. **podido**.
PRES. IND. **puedo, puedes, puede, podemos, podéis, pueden.**
PRES. SUBJ. **pueda, puedas, pueda, podamos, podáis, puedan.**
IMPF. IND. **podía**, etc.; FUT. IND. **podré**, etc.; COND. **podría**, etc.
PRET. IND. **pude, pudiste, pudo, pudimos, pudisteis, pudieron.**
IMPF. SUBJS. **pudiese**, etc.; **pudiera**, etc.; FUT. SUBJ. **pudiere** etc.
IMPERATIVES (*lacking*).

67.   Venir, *to come*

PRES. PART. **viniendo**; PAST PART. **venido**.
PRES. IND. **vengo, vienes, viene,** venimos, venís, **vienen.**
PRES. SUBJ. **venga, vengas, venga, vengamos, vengáis, vengan.**
IMPF. IND. **venía**, etc.; FUT. IND. **vendré**, etc.; COND. **vendría**, etc.
PRET. IND. **vine, viniste, vino, vinimos, vinisteis, vinieron.**
IMPF. SUBJS. **viniese**, etc.; **viniera**, etc.; FUT. SUBJ. **viniere**, etc.
IMPERATIVES **ven**, venid.

IDIOMS

68. *No poder más*   Not to be able to endure (stand) more, be worn out

No puedo más.   I cannot endure (stand) any more, I am worn out.

69. *No poder menos de*   To do no less than, cannot
       (+ *infinitive*)   help (+ *present participle*)

En la Mezquita de Córdoba

El Patio de los Leones en la Alhambra

No pudo menos de venderlo.   He could do no less than sell it, *or,* He could not help selling it.

70. *Por eso*
   Por lo tanto   Accordingly, therefore
   Por consiguiente

No veo bien, por eso (*or* **por lo tanto** *or* **por consiguiente**) **tengo que ponerme anteojos.**
I do not see well, accordingly I have to put on glasses.

A

Granada, 15 de julio de 19—.

Querido amigo:

Ahora estoy en Granada, antigua capital del último reino de los moros de España, en donde quedan todavía grandes monumentos de su civilización, sobre todo la Alhambra, palacio maravilloso de sus reyes. Desde una ventana de 5 mi habitación en la casa de huéspedes puedo ver unas torres de la Alhambra, y a la vez, algunas cimas de la Sierra Nevada cubiertas de nieve. Esta ciudad tiene un clima muy bueno en los meses de julio y agosto, porque no hace tanto calor en el verano como en Córdoba y en Sevilla. 10 Es mejor ir a Sevilla para pasar los meses de enero, febrero y marzo, en los cuales hace frío aquí.

Vd. querrá saber lo que hago cada día. Pues bien, me levanto a las siete o a las siete y media, y me desayuno a las ocho. A las nueve menos cuarto en punto viene el 15 Profesor Juan Morales, quien me da lecciones sobre asuntos comerciales. Los martes y los jueves no viene el profesor. No dedicamos toda la hora a asuntos comerciales, porque hablamos a menudo de la literatura española. Después de la lección suelo pasearme por la ciudad, o subir a la Alham- 20 bra. Me gusta ir a la magnífica Sala de los Embajadores, edificada por Yusuf primero, en la primera mitad del siglo trece, o al Patio de los Leones, construído en el reinado de Mohamed quinto, a fines del siglo trece. Tengo que volver

a casa para el almuerzo a las doce y media. Por la tarde
voy a la biblioteca de la universidad, y salgo a menudo
para tomar helados en un café. Vd. no sabrá a qué hora
comemos. La comida se sirve a las ocho y media de la
5 noche, y le aseguro que siempre tengo mucha hambre antes
de esa hora.

Esta mañana mi profesor me dijo que me había traído
unas facturas que calcular. Por consiguiente me puse a
multiplicar y a sumar como un niño de doce años, pero al
10 fin dije: — ¡ Ay, señor ! hoy no puedo más con estas facturas.
Quiero salir para andar por la ciudad. — El profesor no
pudo menos de consentir.

Pienso quedarme en Granada quince días más, y el
primero de agosto iré a Madrid. Creo poder escribirle de
15 aquí una o dos veces más.

Soy todo de Vd.

LUIS

B

I. *Cuestionario*

1. ¿ En qué ciudad está Luis ahora ?   2. ¿ Por qué es
famosa la ciudad de Granada ?   3. ¿ Qué puede ver Luis
desde su habitación ?   4. ¿ Qué clima tiene Granada ?
5. ¿ Qué estación del año es más agradable en Sevilla ?
6. ¿ A qué hora se desayuna Luis ?   7. ¿ Quién viene a
las nueve menos cuarto ?   8. ¿ Qué lecciones tiene Luis ?
9. ¿ Qué hace Luis después de las lecciones ?   10. ¿ Quiénes
edificaron la Sala de los Embajadores, y el Patio de los
Leones ?   11. ¿ A qué hora se sirve la comida ?   12. ¿ Le
gustan a Luis las facturas ?

II. *Temas*

1. Granada, antigua capital
de los moros.
2. La vista desde la habitación de Luis.
3. El clima de Granada, y el de Sevilla.
4. Las lecciones de Luis.

5. Los paseos de Luis antes
   y después del almuerzo.
6. Los reyes moros que cons-
   truyeron ciertas partes
   de la Alhambra.

7. La Sala de los Embaja-
   dores.
8. Las horas del desayuno,
   del almuerzo, y de la
   comida.

9. Las facturas del profesor.

C

MARY ANDERSON (to John Clark, Louis's friend). — Good
afternoon, Mr. Clark. Is Louis here? He always comes
late. Will he come within fifteen or twenty minutes, at
least? . . . Where did you go this morning?

JOHN. — I went to the Alhambra at half past seven 5
exactly. The buildings are open during the months of
April, May, June, July, and August from eight o'clock in
the morning until noon, and from half past one to five
o'clock in the afternoon. Accordingly, I couldn't help
waiting. The guide had just arrived. He said that I could [1] 10
enter at a quarter-past eight. I went later with the guide
through many magnificent halls; — the Ambassadors' Hall,
built by Joseph First in the first half of the thirteenth
century, the Court of the Lions, constructed in the reign
of Mohámed Fifth, and many other halls. I was 15
tired; I could stand no more. Do you know that the
" Catholic Kings " (king and queen), Ferdinand Fifth and
Isabella, the daughter of John Second of Aragon, came to
Granada on January 2, 1492, the same year that Christopher
Columbus discovered America? 20

MARY. — I never liked history. . . But, tell me, can you
count well in Spanish? I went to the market this morning with Mrs. Mendoza, the landlady of our boarding-
house. We bought six pounds and a [2] half of coffee, half
a [2] box of oranges, three quarters of a box of pears, and 25
other things. Here is the bill: 64 pesetas $+$ 36 pesetas $= 100$

---

[1] Conditional tense.   [2] Omit a.

pesetas; 100 pesetas — 12 pesetas (the pears were no good) = 88 pesetas. We paid half [1] of the bill: 88 pesetas ÷ by 2 = 44 pesetas. Is it correct? You are a mathematician. Tell me.

D

Drill

1. He was able to come Friday, at twenty minutes of seven in the morning. 2. The sun was shining when they were coming to the class. 3. They had been studying for an hour and a half, at least. 4. Shall we be able to study on July fourth? 5. We have to learn the first paragraph of the third chapter on page thirty-three. 6. I can stand no more; let us go. 7. The professor did not come last Tuesday. 8. Accordingly, we were not able to learn anything. 9. Last night it was moonlight from ten o'clock until half past one. 10. It was in the month of December; it was cold, and he was worn out. 11. His cousins came to the United States in the nineteenth century. 12. We came to New York, June 13, 1903. 13. Alphonso XIII, the king of Spain, was born May 11, 1886. 14. Come here,[2] and try to write this arithmetical problem. 15. $4 \times 6 = 24 \div 3 = 8 + 14 = 22 - 22 = 0$. 16. They are coming; shall you come? 17. Can you tell me how old she is? 18. I do not believe that she is (*pres. subj.*) twenty-one years old.

---

[1] *the half.*   [2] **acá** (§ **108,** footnote 1).

EXERCISE VII

Personal Pronouns

71. The table of personal pronouns is as follows:—

		Conjunctive (used as subject or object of a verb)			Disjunctive or Prepositional (used as object of a preposition)
		SUBJECT	INDIRECT OBJECT	DIRECT OBJECT	
	1.	yo	me	me	mí [3]
	2.	tú	te	te	ti [3]
Singular	3.	él	le	le, lo [2]	él
		ella	le	la	ella
		usted	le	le, lo, la	usted
		ello [1]	(wanting)	lo [1]	ello
		(wanting)	se	se	sí [3]
	1.	nosotros, -as	nos	nos	nosotros, -as
	2.	vosotros, -as	os	os	vosotros, -as
Plural	3.	ellos	les	los	ellos
		ellas	les	las	ellas
		ustedes	les	los, las	ustedes
			(neuter plural wanting)		
		(wanting)	se	se	sí [3]

72. The personal pronouns, except **usted (V., Vd., Ud.)** and **ustedes (V.V., Vds., Uds.)**, are usually omitted as subjects of verbs unless required for emphasis or clearness. **Usted** and **ustedes,** as subjects, are ordinarily used only once in the same sentence.

Tengo (Tenemos) muchas peras.	I have (We have) many pears.
(Emphasis) **Él tiene muchos cuadros pero yo no tengo ninguno.**	*He* has many pictures, but *I* do not have any.
(Clearness) **Yo (Él, Ella) escribía.**	I (He, She) was writing.
Usted dice que estudia mucho.	You say that you study much.

---

[1] The neuter forms **ello** and **lo** are limited in use. They refer to a whole idea or phrase, but never to a definite noun. **Ello es que no trabaja,** *The fact is that he does not work.* **No lo creo,** *I do not believe it.*

[2] There is a strong tendency to use **le** for masculine persons and **lo** for masculine things. The English neuters *it* and *them* must be expressed by **la** and **las** when they refer to things which are feminine in Spanish.

[3] The pronouns **mí, ti,** and **sí,** when used with the preposition **con** become **conmigo, contigo,** and **consigo.**

73. The ordinary form of direct address (the word *you*) is expressed by **usted** and **ustedes** (formal speech) used with the third person of the verb. The forms **tú** and **vosotros,** used with the second person of the verb, are employed in addressing near relatives, intimate friends, servants, and animals.

> Señor García, Vd. tiene mucho que hacer.
> *Mr. Garcia, you have a great deal to do.*
> Juan, hijo mío, (tú) no me has escrito a menudo.
> *John, my son, you have not written to me often.*

74. Sentence position of conjunctive object pronouns.[1] — 1. Object pronouns regularly precede the verb governing them, and in the case of compound tenses, they immediately precede the auxiliary **haber.**[2]

Le vi y le hablé.	I saw him and spoke to him.
Les he dado muchas cosas.	I have given them many things.

2. Object pronouns follow and are attached to infinitives, present participles, affirmative imperatives, and subjunctives used as affirmative imperatives.

Voy a escribirle, diciéndole esto.	I am going to write to him, telling him this.
Dámelo ahora.	Give it to me now.
Dígame Vd. lo que ha hecho.	Tell me what you have done.

(*a*) When an infinitive or present participle is used directly after another verb, the object pronouns are placed either before or after the complete verbal expression.

Quiero verlos, *or*, Los quiero ver.	I wish to see them.
Estoy escribiéndole, *or*, Le estoy escribiendo.	I am writing to him.

---

[1] Conjunctive object pronouns are frequently used redundantly with nouns. **Le dió al empleado un premio,** *He gave the employee a reward.*

[2] No pronoun may intervene between **haber** and the past participle, unless **haber** is in the infinitive or present participle. See § 4, 1, footnote 4.

3. The indirect object precedes the direct object. The reflexive pronoun **se**, however, whether direct or indirect object, precedes any other object pronoun.

Nos lo da.	He gives it to us.
Quiere dárnoslo.	He wishes to give it to us.
No se le dijo nada.	Nothing was said to him.

(*a*) **Se** (*not reflexive in this use*) is employed for the indirect object forms **le** and **les,** in case **lo, la, los,** or **las** follows.

Se lo doy (se lo *for* le lo *or* les lo).	I give it to him, *or,* to them.
Se las doy (se las *for* le las *or* les las).	I give them to him, *or,* to them.

75. The disjunctive (prepositional) pronouns are used: [1] —

1. As the object of a preposition.

Primero patiné con ella, y después con él.	I skated first with her, and afterward with him.

2. In addition to object conjunctive pronouns, for clearness or emphasis.[2]

Le hablé a él, a ella, a Vd.	I spoke to him, to her, to you.
Les hablé a ellos, a ellas, a Vds.	I spoke to them (*m.*), to them (*f.*), to you.
Vd. me ve a mí,[3] **pero no le ve a él.**	You see me, but you do not see him.

3. After verbs of motion.

Los niños vendrán a mí.	The children will come to me.
Su hijo corrió a él.	His son ran to him.

---

[1] In case there are two pronoun objects of a verb, and the direct object is in the first or second person, the indirect object is expressed by the disjunctive form. The order is then as in English. **Me presentó a ella,** *He introduced me to her.* BUT: **Me los presentó,** *He introduced them to me.*

[2] For the use of **mismo** for emphasis, see § **132.**

[3] For still greater emphasis, the sentence order **A mí me ve Vd.** may be used.

VERBS

76.   Saber,[1] *to know*

Pres. Part. sabiendo; Past Part. sabido.

Pres. Ind. **sé,** sabes, sabe, sabemos, sabéis, saben.

Pres. Subj. **sepa, sepas, sepa, sepamos, sepáis, sepan.**

Impf. Ind. sabía, etc.; Fut. Ind. **sabré,** etc.; Cond. **sabría,** etc.

Pret. Ind. **supe, supiste, supo, supimos, supisteis, supieron.**

Impf. Subjs. **supiese,** etc.; **supiera,** etc.; Fut. Subj. **supiere,** etc.

Imperatives sabe, sabed.

77.   Dar, *to give*

Pres. Part. dando; Past Part. dado.

Pres. Ind. **doy,** das, da, damos, dais, dan.

Pres. Subj. **dé,** des, **dé,** demos, deis, den.

Impf. Ind. daba, etc.; Fut. Ind. daré, etc.; Cond. daría, etc.

Pret. Ind. **di, diste, dió, dimos, disteis, dieron.**

Impf. Subjs. **diese,** etc.; **diera,** etc.; Fut. Subj. **diere,** etc.

Imperatives da, dad.

78.   Volver, *to return*

Pres. Part. volviendo; Past Part. **vuelto.**

Pres. Ind. **vuelvo, vuelves, vuelve,** volvemos, volvéis, **vuelven.**

Pres. Subj. **vuelva, vuelvas, vuelva,** volvamos, volváis, **vuelvan.**

Impf. Ind. volvía, etc.; Fut. Ind. volveré, etc.; Cond. volvería, etc.

Saber	Conocer
[1] (a) To know, have knowledge of (*things*).	(a) To know, be acquainted with (*persons and things*).
(b) Governs clauses.	(b) Cannot govern clauses.

Conozco al Sr. López, y sé que está allí.

I know Mr. Lopez, and I know that he is there.

Saber	Poder
(c) (+ *infinitive*) can, know how.	(c) (+ *infinitive*) can, be able.

Sabe escribir español, pero no puede escribir hoy.

He can (knows how to) write Spanish, but he cannot (is not able to) write to-day.

PRET. IND. volví, volviste, volvió, volvimos, volvisteis, volvieron.
IMPF. SUBJS. volviese, etc.; volviera, etc.; FUT. SUBJ. volviere,
etc.
IMPERATIVES **vuelve,** volved.

IDIOMS

79. *Volver a* (+ *infinitive*)   To (*infinitive*) again

Volvió a hablar.   He spoke again.

80. *De vez* (*or cuando*)   From time to time, now and
en cuando   then

Los vemos de vez (cuando)   We see them from time to time.
en cuando.

81. *Cosa de* }
Poco más o menos }   About, approximately

Vimos cosa de veinte personas, *or*
Vimos veinte personas poco más o menos.
We saw about twenty persons.

A

Granada, 20 de julio de 19—.

Querido Alberto:

De vez en cuando recibo una carta de los Estados Unidos,
pero mis amigos no me dicen nada de los asuntos comerciales
y políticos. Por eso, hágame el favor de enviarme al menos
algunos periódicos. Los leeré con mucho gusto. Podré 5
enviarle a Vd. periódicos españoles, si los quiere.

No le dije en mi última carta que no pude ver a mi amigo,
Roberto Gómez, cuando llegué. Fuí a su casa, y un criado
me dijo que no sabía donde estaba, pero creía que pronto
volvería. Le di al criado una tarjeta con mi dirección, y 10
me dijo que se la daría a don Roberto a su vuelta.

Ayer, cuando el Profesor Morales salía de mi habitación
a las diez, llegó mi amigo Roberto. Saludó al profesor, a
quien conoce, y acudió a mí. — ¡ Qué sorpresa ! Yo creía

que no llegaría Vd. a Granada antes de agosto. ¿ Hace
muchos días que está aquí ? ¿ Cómo está ? — Hace ocho
días poco más o menos que llegué — le contesté. — ¿ Qué
ha visto Vd. ? ¿ Ha ido a la Alhambra y a la catedral ? —
5 Por supuesto que ya las he visto, y quiero volver a verlas.
En la catedral me gusta sobre todo la capilla real con la
tumba de Fernando e Isabel. Toda la Alhambra me
gusta.

Anoche fuí a ver a Roberto. Estaba solo en la sala
10 cuando entré. Cuando su madre llegó, Roberto me presentó
a ella, diciéndole que era yo su mejor amigo norteamericano.
— Nos hace Vd. un gran favor en venir a vernos — me dijo
la señora. Le contesté que me hacía más favor ella en
recibirme en su casa. Entonces llegó la hermana menor de
15 Roberto, y éste me la presentó. Le dije que comprendía
bien el entusiasmo de Roberto por volver a vivir con su
familia, puesto que tenía una madre tan graciosa y una
hermanita tan encantadora. — Roberto, es Vd. dichoso.
Yo no tengo hermana, y hace ya algunos años que murieron
20 mis padres.

Pronto llegaron el padre y el hermano mayor de Roberto.
Pasé unas horas muy agradables, y a las once regresé a mi
habitación, acompañado de Roberto.

Trate Vd. de enviarme pronto los periódicos americanos.
25 Quedo como siempre

Su afmo. amigo
Luis

B

I. *Cuestionario*

1. ¿ Qué recibía Luis de los Estados Unidos ? 2. ¿ Qué
otras cosas quería recibir ? 3. ¿ Halló Luis a su amigo
Roberto en casa cuando llegó ? 4. ¿ Qué le dijo a Luis
el criado ? 5. ¿ Qué le dió Luis al criado ? 6. ¿ Cuándo
llegó Roberto a la casa de huéspedes de Luis ? 7. ¿ Qué

preguntas le hizo Roberto? 8. ¿Qué había visto Luis en Granada? 9. ¿A quiénes conoció Luis en casa de su amigo? 10. ¿Volvió solo Luis a su habitación?

II. *Temas*

1. Las cartas de los Estados Unidos.
2. Los periódicos.
3. La primera visita de Luis a casa de Roberto.
4. La llegada de Roberto a la habitación de Luis.
5. Las preguntas de Roberto.
6. Las cosas de Granada que le gustaban a Luis.
7. La segunda visita de Luis a casa de Roberto.
8. La familia de Roberto.
9. La familia de Luis.
10. La vuelta de Luis a su habitación.

C

MARY (*in the dining-room of the boarding-house*). — Louis, Mrs. Mendoza is there near the table; go to her, and give her the newspaper. You are reading it all the time. Then come to us and tell us the sum of this bill. Mrs. Mendoza gave it to me. I went with her to the market this morn- 5 ing. My mother could not go with me. Mother, give it to him; I cannot give it to him, myself.[1] . . . Mr. Clark, you know my mother, do you not?

JOHN. — Yes, Miss Anderson, I have known her for two days. Louis introduced me to her day before yesterday . . . 10 Your bill has no mistakes in it. It amounts to about ninety pesetas. Louis is reading the newspaper but I shall give it (*the bill*) to him.

MRS. MENDOZA. — Do not give it to him, John. I have something more interesting. Come here, ladies, and I 15 shall give you some [2] coffee. *You* like it very much; *I* do not like it. I drink it from time to time, but I prefer chocolate with sugar. John, never have I seen you drink [3] chocolate. Miss Anderson, give it to him, and take half a cup

---

[1] yo misma, § 132.   [2] Omit.   [3] Use tomar.

yourself; then he cannot help drinking it. . . Louis, do you not feel like drinking [1] something too?

LOUIS. — I shall be very glad to do so.[2] I have just drunk a cup of coffee with Captain Colín, but I am still
5 thirsty. Do you know him? I shall see him again at half past four, and John and I are going with him to see the Gipsies in their Cave Dwellings (**Cuevas**). He says that they have been in Granada since the year 1532. He says, also, that the dances of the Gipsy girls are charming.
10 What good luck! . . . I mean, for [3] John; such a thing, of course, does not please *me*.

D

Drill

1. We go to the Spanish Club, Thursdays, at a quarter of seven.   2. Are you acquainted with Miss Jackson, the president of the Club?   3. Yes, Mr. Allen introduced me to her.   4. Does she give us coffee often at the meetings?   5. She never gives it to us.   6. She gives us only tea.   7. She gave it to me yesterday in her home.   8. Tea is no good.   9. *She* likes it, *I* do not like it.   10. Good evening, Mr. Smith, I shall give you some tea.   11. Do not give it to him, Miss Jackson, give it to me.   12. Please give me about half a [4] cup.   13. Thank you; I shall see you again.   14. Louis will return with me from time to time, and we shall drink with you.   15. I could not help drinking it, Louis.   16. Why has Miss Jackson not returned?   17. She did not know a certain Spanish word, and is looking for it in the dictionary.   18. You did not know the irregular verbs, yesterday.   19. Do you know them to-day, and shall you know them to-morrow?   20. I can sing Spanish songs, but I am tired and cannot sing to-night.

---

[1] Use **tomar**   [2] **lo.**.   [3] **para**   [4] Omit.

EXERCISE VIII

Comparison of Adjectives and Adverbs — Formation of Adverbs

82. Comparisons of inequality. — The comparative of inequality is regularly formed by placing **más** or **menos** before the positive form of adjectives and adverbs. The superlative of adjectives is formed [1] by placing the definite article or the possessive pronoun before the comparative form. [2] The superlative form of adverbs [3] is usually the same as the comparative.

POSITIVE	COMPARATIVE	SUPERLATIVE
Adjective **fácil**	**más (menos) fácil**	**el (la) más (menos) fácil**
		los (las) más (menos) fáciles
Adverb **despacio**	**más (menos) despacio**	(*same as comparative*)

De ese modo será más fácil.	In that way it will be easier.
Esta lección es la más fácil del libro.	This lesson is the easiest in [4] the book.
Cuando habla más despacio, le comprendo.	When he speaks more slowly, I understand him.

83. Four adjectives and four adverbs are compared irregularly:

ADJECTIVES

grande	mayor	el (la) mayor	bueno	mejor	el (la) mejor
pequeño	menor	el (la) menor	malo	peor	el (la) peor

---

[1] The absolute superlative (*not denoting any real comparison*) is expressed by placing **muy** before the adjective, or by adding the suffix -**ísimo** to it. It is expressed in English by *very* or *exceedingly* with the adjective. **Útil,** *useful,* **muy útil** or **utilísimo,** *very (exceedingly) useful.* Note that **muchísimo** (not **muy mucho**) is used as the absolute superlative of **mucho.**

[2] The sentence position of the superlative form of an adjective is regularly after its noun, and the accompanying article precedes the noun. **La casa más grande,** *the largest house.*

[3] The superlatives of adverbs may have the neuter article **lo** before them, in case they are followed by a word or phrase expressing possibility. **Vino lo más pronto posible,** *He came as soon as possible.*

[4] After superlatives, the word *in* is expressed by **de.**

mucho	más	bien [1]	mejor
poco	menos	mal	peor

(a) **Grande** and **pequeño** are compared both regularly and irregularly. When they are compared regularly, they refer to size; when they are compared irregularly, they usually refer to age or rank.

La pintura grande es buena, pero la más pequeña es la mejor de la colección.	The large painting is good, but the smallest one is the best in the collection.
Es mi hermana menor.	She is my youngest sister.

84. Spanish equivalents of the word *than*. — 1. The word *than* in a comparison of inequality is expressed by **que.**

Carlos es más pobre que su hermano.	Charles is poorer than his brother.
Aquel hombre tiene menos dinero que su primo.	That man has less money than his cousin.

2. Before cardinal numbers *than* is expressed by **de** in affirmative statements, while **que** is more usual in negative statements.

Hemos visto más de cien estudiantes.	We have seen more than one hundred students.
No hay más que diez panes en la cesta.	There are only (no more than) ten loaves of bread in the basket.

3. Before a clause, when the comparison is based upon a noun of the principal clause, *than* is **del que, de la que, de los que, de las que,** agreeing in gender and number with this noun. When the comparison is with the whole idea in the previous clause, which usually terminates in an adjective or an adverb, *than* is **de lo que** (*invariable*).

---

[1] **Más bien** occurs with the meaning of *rather.* **Parece perezoso más bien que cansado,** *He seems lazy rather than tired.*

Tenía más dinero del que me dió.	He had more money than he gave me.
Me trajeron más libros de los que me habían prometido.	They brought me more books than they had promised me.
Es más fuerte de lo que creían.	He is stronger than they believed.

85. Comparisons of equality. — 1. In comparing adjectives and adverbs, *as (so) . . . as* is expressed by **tan . . . como.**

Es tan trabajador como su hermana.	He is as diligent as his sister.
No leo tan bien como él.	I do not read so well as he.

2. In comparing nouns, *as (so) much (many) . . . as* is expressed by **tanto (-os), tanta (-as) . . . como.**

Vd. no tenía tanto café como yo.	You did not have so much coffee as I.
No he comido tantas peras como él.	I have not eaten so many pears as he.

3. In comparing clauses, *the more (less) . . . the more (less)* is expressed by **cuanto** [1] **más (menos) . . . tanto** [1] **más (menos).**

Cuanto más gana, tanto más desea.	The more he earns, the more he wants.
Cuanto menos sabe, tanto más debe trabajar.	The less he knows, the more he ought to work.

86. Formation of adverbs. — Many adverbs may be derived from adjectives by adding **-mente** [2] to the feminine form of the adjective.

Fácil, *easy,* fácilmente, *easily;* rápido, *rapid,* rápidamente, *rapidly.*

Podemos verlo fácilmente	We can see it easily.
Lo harán rápidamente.	They will do it rapidly.

---

[1] **Cuanto** may be replaced by **mientras,** and **tanto** may be dropped entirely from the second member of the comparison. **Mientras más gana, más desea,** *The more he earns, the more he wants.*

[2] When two adverbs ending in **-mente** are used in succession, the last one only retains the **-mente**; the first one has the ending of the feminine of the adjective. **Hace su trabajo rápida y fácilmente,** *He does his work rapidly and easily.*

VERBS

87. Ver, *to see*

Pres. Part. **viendo**; Past Part. **visto**.
Pres. Ind. **veo, ves, ve, vemos, veis, ven**.
Pres. Subj. **vea, veas, vea, veamos, veáis, vean**.
Impf. Ind. **veía, veías, veía, veíamos, veíais, veían**.
Fut. Ind. **veré**, etc.; Cond. **vería**, etc.
Pret. Ind. **vi, viste, vió, vimos, visteis, vieron**.
Impf. Subjs. **viese**, etc.; **viera**, etc.; Fut. Subj. **viere**, etc.
Imperatives **ve**, ved.

88. Pensar, *to think*

Pres. Part. **pensando**; Past Part. **pensado**.
Pres. Ind. **pienso, piensas, piensa, pensamos, pensáis, piensan**.
Pres. Subj. **piense, pienses, piense, pensemos, penséis, piensen**.
Impf. Ind. **pensaba**, etc.; Fut. Ind. **pensaré**, etc.; Cond.
   pensaría, etc.
Pret. Ind. **pensé, pensaste, pensó, pensamos, pensasteis,
   pensaron**.
Impf. Subjs. **pensase**, etc.; **pensara**, etc.; Fut. Subj. **pensare**,
   etc.
Imperatives **piensa**, pensad.

89. traer, *to bring*

Pres. Part. **trayendo**; Past Part. **traído**.
Pres. Ind. **traigo**, traes, trae, traemos, traéis, traen.
Pres. Subj. **traiga, traigas, traiga, traigamos, traigáis, traigan**.
Impf. Ind. **traía**, etc.; Fut. Ind. **traeré**, etc.; Cond. **traería**, etc.
Pret. Ind. **traje, trajiste, trajo, trajimos, trajisteis, trajeron**.
Impf. Subjs. **trajese**, etc.; **trajera**, etc.; Fut. Subj. **trajere**, etc.
Imperatives **trae**, traed.

IDIOMS

90. *En vez (or lugar) de*   Instead of

Comen en vez de trabajar.   They are eating instead of
   working.

VISTA DESDE LA ALHAMBRA SOBRE EL ALBAICÍN

El Rey de los gitanos, Granada

91. *Ser aficionado a*

Es aficionado a la música.

To be fond of

He is fond of music.

92. *Cuanto antes* }
    Tan pronto como posible }

As soon as possible

Iremos cuanto antes (tan pronto como posible).

We shall go as soon as possible.

A

Granada, 30 de julio de 19—.

Sra. Doña Lucía Holmes,
   Filadelfia,
      Pa.

Estimada señora:

Hoy estoy sentado con papel y pluma cerca de una ventana de la gran Sala de los Embajadores de la Alhambra, desde donde veo las montañas, y pienso en Vd., tan artística como aficionada a todo lo bello. Le ruego que venga a 5 España el verano próximo en vez de ir a Italia. Sería difícil encontrar un palacio más encantador que la Alhambra. Es verdad que las salas son menos grandes de lo que esperaba; sin embargo con sus columnas delgadas, sus inscripciones árabes y sus arabescos enredados parece 10 seguramente el mejor ejemplo de la arquitectura árabe. La mezquita árabe de Córdoba con sus ochocientas columnas me ha entusiasmado, pero la Alhambra es delicadísima y me gusta más, sobre todo el Patio de los Leones. Parece la más hermosa creación de los ensueños del artista. Es 15 mucho más hermosa de lo que yo había creído. Vd. habrá leído tantos libros como yo acerca de los edificios de España, y estoy seguro de que no hay nada más maravilloso en este país que la Alhambra. Vd. debe verla. Cuanto más la veo, tanto más tiempo quiero quedarme 20 aquí. La creo digna de la mayor admiración.

Ayer quise comprar fotografías de la Alhambra, y entré en una tienda donde las había visto. Me trajo el dependiente más fotografías de las que pude mirar en media hora. Ciertamente me trajo más de doscientas. Al fin
5 escogí veinte y cuatro de las mejores, y salí contentísimo de la tienda. Tendré mucho gusto en enseñárselas a Vd. cuando vuelva a los Estados Unidos.

Al salir de la tienda con las fotografías, vi a mi amigo, Roberto Gómez, y quise enseñárselas inmediatamente.
10 Le gustaron mucho. Cuando le dije que pensaba marcharme para Madrid pasado mañana, no quiso permitirlo, sino que trató de hacerme permanecer en Granada al menos ocho días más. Prometió ir conmigo cuanto antes a ver los bailes de los gitanos del Albaicín, y hacer una excursión
15 a las montañas. Sin embargo tengo que irme. Será con un suspiro como el del último rey moro al salir de Granada.

Esperando contarle personalmente otras muchas cosas de interés cuando la vea en América, quedo siempre

Su atento amigo y S. S.

Luis Oliver

47

B

I. *Cuestionario*

1. ¿Dónde estaba Luis, cuando escribió la carta? 2. ¿Qué veía desde las ventanas? 3. ¿Qué le rogó a la Sra. Holmes? 4. ¿Cuál le gustaba más a Luis, la mezquita de Córdoba o la Alhambra de Granada? 5. ¿Qué adornos hay en la arquitectura árabe? 6. ¿Cuánto tiempo quería Luis quedarse en Granada? 7. ¿Qué compró? 8. ¿A quién enseñó sus compras? 9. ¿Qué prometió hacer Roberto? 10. ¿Cómo saldrá Luis de Granada?

II. *Temas*

1. La Sala de los Embaja-
dores.
2. El viaje de la Sra. Holmes
a España.
3. La mezquita de Córdoba.
4. Las salas de la Alhambra
y el Patio de los Leones.
5. La admiración de Luis.

6. Las fotografías en la
tienda.
7. Las fotografías y Ro-
berto Gómez.
8. La salida de Luis para
Madrid.
9. Las promesas de Ro-
berto.

10. Lo que contará Luis a la Sra. Holmes.

C

MARY. — Louis, do you intend to visit the park of the
Alhambra again? You must see it the next time at night.[1]
John and I went last evening. It was moonlight, and the
park was very beautiful with its large trees. Almost all
of the trees are elms, brought from England by Wellington 5
in 1812. They are larger than the elms in our city. The
largest ones are as large as the elms in Washington.

LOUIS. — Instead of elms in the moonlight, I saw some
Gipsy girls. I liked them exceedingly. They were pretty,
and they danced gracefully and happily. I thought of you, 10
from time to time, because you are so fond of dancing.
The smallest children in the band begged continually. I
gave them more than twenty of those coins of five centimos
which are called [2] colloquially "little dogs." The larger
coins of ten centimos are called [2] "big dogs." The more I 15
gave them, the more they wanted. Finally I could stand
no more, and I told them to go away.[3] The youngest and
prettiest Gipsy girl talked with me a long while. She
did not want to talk with Captain Martin but with me

---

[1] **de noche** as opposed to **de día,** *by day.*   [2] **se llaman** (§ 131, 4).
[3] Imperf. subj., § 140, 1, footnote 2.

because I was an American, and, of course, exceedingly rich.

MARY. — Are you not ashamed to talk of Gipsies instead of the Alhambra? . . . You have probably read the wonder-
5 ful *Tales of the Alhambra* by Washington Irving. His stories of the Alhambra are the best ones written in English. The more I read them, the more they please me. We must read, this winter, all the works of Washington Irving. My mother says that she is going to give them to me as
10 soon as possible. Therefore, she will give me less money for my birthday than she has promised. It doesn't matter. Girls prefer books to candy.

D

Drill

1. I saw more than a hundred students at the picnic yesterday. 2. There were only (no more than) four professors. 3. We brought coffee, ice cream, and other things. 4. Men like ice cream, as dessert, instead of fruit. 5. The men bought more things than they could bring. 6. The girls brought as many things as the men. 7. The men ate more than they brought. 8. The less they bring, the more they eat. 9. Do you intend to help us, John? Here is the package of coffee. 10. Give it to him, Mary; do not give it to me. 11. He has less than the others are bringing. 12. Everybody is working rapidly and happily. 13. I like exceedingly the trees in the park. 14. They are as large as the elms near the University. 15. Have you ever seen the largest elm in the park? 16. I shall see it as soon as possible. 17. We shall think often of this picnic. 18. Think of me when you see (*pres. subj.*) the picture. 19. I hope that you may think (*pres. subj.*) of me often. 20. I have as much money as the professor. 21. I do not think that he is (*pres. subj.*) exceedingly rich.

EXERCISE IX

Possessive Adjectives and Pronouns

93. Possessive adjectives and pronouns. — 1. The table of possessive adjectives is as follows: —

Before noun		After noun			
SINGULAR	PLURAL	SINGULAR		PLURAL	
		Mas.	*Fem.*	*Mas.*	*Fem.*
mi	mis	mío	mía	míos	mías *my*
tu	tus	tuyo	tuya	tuyos	tuyas *your* (familiar, sing.)
su	sus	suyo	suya	suyos	suyas *his, her, its, their,*
					your (formal, sing. and pl.)

Before or after noun

SINGULAR		PLURAL		
Mas.	*Fem.*	*Mas.*	*Fem.*	
nuestro	nuestra	nuestros	nuestras	*our*
vuestro	vuestra	vuestros	vuestras	*your*
				(familiar, pl.)

2. The table of possessive pronouns [1] is as follows: —

SINGULAR		PLURAL		
Mas.	*Fem.*	*Mas.*	*Fem.*	
el mío	la mía	los míos	las mías	*mine*
el tuyo	la tuya	los tuyos	las tuyas	*yours* (familiar, sing.)
el suyo	la suya	los suyos	las suyas	*his, hers, its, theirs,*
				yours (formal, sing. and pl.)
el nuestro	la nuestra	los nuestros	las nuestras	*ours*
el vuestro	la vuestra	los vuestros	las vuestras	*yours* (familiar, pl.)

94. Agreement. — In Spanish, the possessive adjectives and pronouns agree with the thing possessed, and not, as in English, with the possessor.

Veo mis plumas y nuestra tinta.	I see my pens and our ink.
El tiene sus cuellos, y yo tengo los míos.	He has his collars, and I have mine.

---

[1] A possessive pronoun used with **ser** usually omits its article, unless emphatic distinction is desired. **Esta caja es mía,** *This box is mine.*

95. A possessive adjective modifying two or more nouns is regularly repeated before each one.

> **Nuestros pañuelos y nuestras corbatas están aquí.**
> Our handkerchiefs and neckties are here.

96. The form of the possessive adjective which precedes the noun occurs more frequently than the form which follows. The latter is used in direct address, for emphasis, or when in English *of mine, of yours,* etc. are used.

Nuestro hijo estaba en Valencia.	Our son used to be in Valencia.
Hija mía, no leas todo el tiempo.	My daughter, do not read all the time.
Un primo mío ha venido.	A cousin of mine has come.

97. Use of the definite article. — The definite article is commonly employed instead of the possessive adjective when referring to clothing or parts of the body, in case there is no doubt concerning the possessor. In case of doubt, an indirect object pronoun is used with the verb.

El niño no quería quitarse el sombrero.	The child did not want to take off his hat.
Carlos tiene una pluma en la mano.	Charles has a pen in his hand.
Me pongo los guantes.	I am putting on my gloves.

(*a*) When the object referred to is a thing in the singular the like of which is possessed by several individuals of a group, a singular noun is generally used in Spanish.

> **Los niños se lavaron la cara.**   The children washed their faces.

98. Uncertainty in meaning may arise in the use of the possessive adjective **su** (**sus**) from the fact that the meaning may be *his, her, its, your* or *their.* When such uncertainty arises, it should be avoided by the use of either one of the methods indicated below:

el lápiz los lápices	de él de ella de usted de ellos de ellas de ustedes	*his* *her* *your*, m. and f. *their*, m. *their*, f. *your*, m. and f.	su lápiz (or) sus lápices	de él de ella de usted de ellos de ellas de ustedes

He visto su (el) lápiz de Vd. — I have seen your pencil.
¿ Dónde están las (sus) plumas de ellos? — Where are their pens?

99. Uncertainty in meaning may arise in the use of the possessive pronouns **el suyo, los suyos, la suya,** and **las suyas** from the fact that any one of these forms may mean *his, hers, its, yours,* or *theirs.* When such uncertainty arises, it should be avoided by the use of the forms indicated in the following table:

For	1. el suyo 2. la suya 3. los suyos 4. las suyas	substitute	1. el 2. la 3. los 4. las	de	él ella usted ellos ellas ustedes	*his* *hers* *yours*, m. and f. *theirs*, m. *theirs*, f. *yours*, m. and f.

Vieron nuestro cuadro y el de ella. — They saw our picture and hers.

Tengo mis anteojos y los de ellos. — I have my spectacles and theirs.

VERBS

100. Salir, *to go out, leave*

Pres. Part. saliendo; Past Part. salido.
Pres. Ind. **salgo,** sales, sale, salimos, salís, salen.
Pres. Subj. **salga, salgas, salga, salgamos, salgáis, salgan.**
Impf. Ind. salía, etc.; Fut. Ind. **saldré,** etc; Cond. **saldría,** etc.
Pret. Ind. salí, saliste, salió, salimos, salisteis, salieron.
Impf. Subjs. saliese, etc.; saliera, etc.; Fut. Subj. saliere, etc.
Imperatives **sal,** salid.

101. Reír, *to laugh*

PRES. PART. **riendo**; PAST PART. **reído**.
PRES. IND. **río, ríes, ríe,** reímos, reís, **ríen**.
PRES. SUBJ. **ría, rías, ría,** riamos, riáis, **rían**.
IMPF. IND. reía, etc.; FUT. IND. reiré, etc.; COND. reiría, etc.
PRET. IND. reí, reíste, **rió,** reímos, reísteis, **rieron**.
IMPF. SUBJS. **riese,** etc.; **riera,** etc.; FUT. SUBJ. **riere,** etc.
IMPERATIVES **ríe,** reíd.

102. Sentir, *to feel, regret*

PRES. PART. **sintiendo**; PAST PART. **sentido**.
PRES. IND. **siento, sientes, siente,** sentimos, sentís, **sienten**.
PRES. SUBJ. **sienta, sientas, sienta, sintamos, sintáis, sientan**.
IMPF. IND. sentía, etc.; FUT. IND. sentiré, etc.; COND. sentiría,
etc.
PRET. IND. sentí, sentiste, **sintió,** sentimos, sentisteis, **sintieron**.
IMPF. SUBJS. **sintiese,** etc.; **sintiera,** etc.; FUT. SUBJ. **sintiere,**
etc.
IMPERATIVES **siente,** sentid.

IDIOMS

103. *Dejar de* (+ *infinitive*)   To fail to, cease to, stop
Nunca dejan de venir.   They never fail to come.
Deje Vd. de hablarme.   Stop talking to me.

104. *En cuanto a*   As for, concerning
En cuanto a mi hermano, no   As for my brother, he will
  saldrá.   not leave.

105. *De repente*   Suddenly
Salieron de repente.   They went out suddenly.

A

Madrid, 4 de agosto de 19—.

Querido Alberto:

Hace dos días que estoy en Madrid. Escribí a Carlos
López, mi amigo, que llegaría a Madrid el primero o el dos

de agosto, y que iría a vivir en la casa de huéspedes de la
Sra. García, calle de la Cruz 15. Al llegar a la casa, me
dijo la patrona que un amigo mío había venido, y que le
había entregado a ella su tarjeta de visita, diciéndole que
volvería al día siguiente. Era una tarjeta de Carlos López. 5
Carlos no dejó de venir, y le recibí con mucha alegría.
Después de hablar cosa de una hora, Carlos propuso ir
conmigo a un teatro. — ¿ Qué clase de teatro le gusta más ?
— me preguntó. — Las comedias de Lope de Vega — contesté sin vacilar. — No estoy de acuerdo con Vd. Las de 10
él son muy buenas, pero hay comedias modernas que me
gustan más. ¿ No conoce Vd. las piezas de Benavente y
las de los hermanos Quintero ? — No las conozco muy bien,
lo cual siento mucho. — ¿ Ha oído Vd. alguna vez una zarzuela moderna ? — No he oído ninguna de ellas. — ¡ Ca- 15
ramba ! Vamos esta noche. Si vamos cuanto antes,
llegaremos para la función de las diez. La función no dura
más que una hora de ordinario.
Acababan de principiar la función cuando entramos.
Dos hombres y dos mujeres cantaban y bailaban a la vez 20
en el escenario. Las voces de los hombres me gustaron,
pero las de las mujeres eran malas. De vez en cuando
hablaban sin cantar, pero yo no entendía bien lo que decían.
A menudo Carlos se reía de los chistes. De repente salió
un bribón, y le cantó sus amores a una de las mujeres. 25
Respondió ella que no los deseaba, y le pidió a uno de los
dos primeros hombres su ayuda contra el bribón. Sobre-
vino una lucha terrible con espadas, mientras gritaban y
cantaban las mujeres. El bribón se cayó muerto, y los
otros actores cantaron una canción de alegría. La música 30
era muy bonita. Salimos del teatro y volvimos a mi casa,
donde tuve que llamar a gritos al sereno, quien llegó al fin,
y me abrió la puerta.
Otro día le escribiré más.

Su afmo. amigo
Luis

B

I. *Cuestionario*

1. ¿ A quién escribió Luis ?   2. ¿ Dónde dijo que viviría en Madrid ?   3. ¿ Qué le dió a Luis la patrona, al llegar él a la casa ?   4. ¿ A dónde propuso ir Carlos ?   5. ¿ Qué comedias le gustaban a Luis ?   6. ¿ A dónde fueron al fin ? 7. ¿ Qué hacían los actores que estaban en el escenario, cuando llegaron los dos amigos ?   8. ¿ Tenían buena voz ? 9. ¿ Cómo terminó la zarzuela ?   10. ¿ Qué hizo el sereno por Luis ?

II. *Temas*

1. La carta de Luis a su amigo, Carlos López.
2. La tarjeta de visita de Carlos.
3. La segunda vez que vino Carlos.
4. Las comedias de Lope de Vega, de Benavente y de los hermanos Quintero.
5. Las zarzuelas.
6. El principio de la función de las diez.
7. Los actores en el escenario.
8. El bribón y su suerte.
9. La música.
10. El sereno.

C

MARY. — Excuse me, Louis, have you seen my gloves ? I saw them on the table in your room, half an hour ago. Mine and my mother's were near yours. Ours are much smaller than yours. You cannot fail to recognize them. 5 Did you put them in your pocket ? I have been looking for them for twenty minutes at least.

LOUIS. — Please stop talking so fast, and put on your glasses. I am sorry to tell you so,[1] but your gloves and handkerchief are on that chair where you put them. Your 10 mother's gloves, and not yours, were on the table with

---

[1] *it.*

mine. You came in suddenly last night, put them on the chair, and went out. What was the matter with you?

MARY. — Do not laugh at [1] me. You are right concerning my mother's gloves, and mine. I see mine on the chair. I went out suddenly last night because I was angry. . . I 5 do not like the night-watchman. The more loudly I call him, the more slowly he comes. He has the keys of four houses, and nobody can enter after eleven o'clock without him. Finally, he comes with his lantern, his staff, and his keys, opens the door, and conducts me to my apartment. 10 He never fails to say "Excuse me, Miss, I came as quickly as possible. I was on the top floor of the next house." John's watchman is older and deafer than ours. John says that he and his companions often remain at night in the street before his door for twenty minutes, with their faces 15 turned toward the stars, calling "Watchman, watchman, watchman" like frogs in a pond.

D

Drill

1. Why did you laugh suddenly, George? 2. Where have you put my green cap? 3. Do not go out without giving it to me. 4. I put mine on the bed near yours. 5. Albert put his on the table. 6. I know that mine is better than his. 7. It is as good as yours, at least. 8. Give it to me; do not fail to do so. 9. I am sorry to tell you so, but Albert is a better friend than you. 10. I know his younger brother and his older sister. 11. Excuse me, Louis, I was not laughing at you. 12. Stop talking so much. 13. As for your hat, it is with Albert's on the table. 14. Put on your hats, my friends, and let us go out. 15. We shall go out as soon as possible. 16. We are going out now; shall we feel the cold? 17. You do not have to put on your overcoats. 18. I am sorry,[2]

---

[1] reírse de (§ 131, 3).   [2] sentir (lo).

but I have less money than I believed.   19. I haven't
more than twenty pesetas.   20. I am going out; they are
laughing at me.   21. We are sorry that you are going
out (*pres. subj.*).   22. They were sorry that he was laughing (*imperf. subj.*) at you.

EXERCISE X

Demonstrative Adjectives and Pronouns — *Para* and *Por*

106. Demonstrative adjectives and pronouns. — The
table of demonstratives is as follows:—

	Adjectives				Pronouns			
	SINGULAR		PLURAL		SINGULAR		PLURAL	
Masc.	este		estos		éste	*this*	éstos	
Fem.	esta	*this*	estas	*these*	ésta	*one,*	éstas	*these*
Neut.	——		——		esto	*this*	——	
Masc.	ese		esos		ése	*that*	ésos	
Fem.	esa	*that*	esas	*those*	ésa	*one,*	ésas	*those*
Neut.	——		——		eso	*that*	——	
Masc.	aquel		aquellos		aquél	*that*	aquéllos	
Fem.	aquella	*that*	aquellas	*those*	aquélla	*one,*	aquéllas	*those*
Neut.	——		——		aquello	*that*	——	

(*a*) The masculine and feminine pronouns have a written
accent on the stressed syllable to distinguish them visually
from the corresponding adjectives.   The neuter pronouns
do not need accents, because there are no neuter adjectives.

Este estudiante fué a la clase, pero aquél quedó en casa.	This student went to class, but that one remained at home.
Estas peras son mejores que ésas.	These pears are better than those.
Esas ideas que tiene Vd. son buenas.	Those ideas which you have are good.
¿ Qué es esto? — Es una silla.	What is this? It is a chair.

107. Agreement. — Demonstrative adjectives agree with their nouns in gender and number and are repeated before each noun to which they refer.

> Estos guisantes y estas judías son buenos.
>
> These peas and beans are good.

108. Meaning of adjectives. — **Este** means *this*, near the speaker.[1]

Ese means *that*, near the person spoken to, or referring to a subject recently mentioned.[1]

Aquel means *that*, remote from both speaker and person spoken to.[1]

> Este anillo de oro es más costoso que ese reloj de plata.
>
> This gold ring is more costly than that silver watch.
>
> Aquel techo es rojo.
>
> That roof is red.

109. The masculine and feminine demonstrative pronouns represent nouns which have been definitely mentioned; the neuter pronouns (**esto, eso, aquello**) represent things not definitely mentioned, or ideas.

> ¿ Qué es aquello? — Es una bandera.
>
> What is that? It is a flag.
>
> No creo eso.
>
> I do not believe that (*something recently mentioned*).

110. Meaning of pronouns. — The pronoun **éste** means *the latter*, and **aquél,** *the former*, in contrasted clauses; **éste,** *the latter*, comes first in the sentence, contrary to English usage.

> Carlos y María han llegado, ésta con dos baúles,
> y aquél con una maleta.
>
> Charles and Mary have arrived, the former with
> a suitcase, and the latter with two trunks.

---

[1] The adverb **aquí,** *here* (*near the speaker*), corresponds to **este**; **ahí,** *there* (*near the person spoken to*), corresponds to **ese**; **allí,** *there* (*remote from both speaker and person spoken to*), corresponds to **aquel**. After verbs of motion, **acá** is commonly used for *here*, and **allá** for *there*.

111. The English demonstrative pronoun is usually expressed in Spanish by the definite article when standing before a phrase beginning with **de,** or before a relative clause.[1]

Mi casa y la de mi padre están en la misma calle.	My house and that of my father (my father's) are in the same street.
La que vió Vd. ayer es mi prima Dolores.	The one (she whom) you saw yesterday is my cousin Dolores.
Lo que dice es sorprendente.	What (that which) he says is surprising.

112. Para, *for, in order to, etc.* is used to express: (1) use, purpose, or destination, (2) a unit or point of future time, (3) proximity of an action (*with infinitive*).

(1) Ésta es una cuchara para sopa.	This is a soup spoon (*spoon for soup*).
Estudiamos para aprender.	We are studying to (in order to) learn.
Esta silla es para Vd.	This chair is for you.
Saldrá para Méjico.	He will leave for Mexico.
(2) Esta lección es para mañana.	This lesson is for to-morrow.
El trabajo estará hecho para las dos.	The work will be done by two o'clock.
(3) Estamos para ir al teatro.	We are about to go to the theater.

113. Por, *for, by, through, etc.,* is used to express: (1) for the sake of, (2) price or exchange, (3) time during which, time of day [2] when the hour is not given, (4) (*with infinitive*) inclination without certainty of accomplishment, (5) place through which, (6) manner or means, (7) physical agency,[3] (8) cause.

---

[1] For treatment of relative pronouns, see § **122,** 3, 4.

[2] For definite time of day, see § **64.**

[3] For the use of **de** with mental action, see § **133,** footnote 3.

(1) **Lo haremos por nuestros amigos.**	We shall do it for (the sake of) our friends.
(2) **Las vendió por una peseta.**	He sold them for one peseta.
Le daré a Vd. esta pluma por ésa.	I shall give you this pen for that one.
(3) **Estaré allí por cuatro meses.**	I shall be there for four months.
Iré mañana por la noche.	I shall go to-morrow night.
(4) **Estamos por ir al teatro.**	We are in favor of going to the theater.
(5) **Pasamos por Zaragoza.**	We passed through Zaragoza.
(6) **Viajaremos por ferrocarril.**	We shall travel by railroad.
(7) **El niño fué castigado por su padre.**	The child was punished by his father.
(8) **Lo hizo por miedo.**	He did it through fear.

VERBS

114. **Pedir,** *to ask, request*

PRES. PART. **pidiendo;** PAST PART. pedido.

PRES. IND. **pido, pides, pide,** pedimos, pedís, **piden.**

PRES. SUBJ. **pida, pidas, pida, pidamos, pidáis, pidan.**

IMPF. IND. pedía, etc.; FUT. IND. pediré, etc.; COND. pediría, etc.

PRET. IND. pedí, pediste, **pidió,** pedimos, pedisteis, **pidieron.**

IMPF. SUBJS. **pidiese,** etc.; **pidiera,** etc.; FUT. SUBJ. **pidiere,** etc.

IMPERATIVES **pide,** pedid.

115. **Servir,** *to serve*

PRES. PART. **sirviendo;** PAST PART. servido.

PRES. IND. **sirvo, sirves, sirve,** servimos, servís, **sirven.**

PRES. SUBJ. **sirva, sirvas, sirva, sirvamos, sirváis, sirvan.**

IMPF. IND. servía, etc.; FUT. IND. serviré, etc.; COND. serviría, etc.

PRET. IND. serví, serviste, **sirvió,** servimos, servisteis, **sirvieron.**

IMPF. SUBJS. **sirviese,** etc.; **sirviera,** etc.; FUT. SUBJ. **sirviere,** etc.

IMPERATIVES **sirve,** servid.

116.   **Vestir,** *to dress*

PRES. PART. **vistiendo;** PAST PART. vestido.

PRES. IND. **visto, vistes, viste,** vestimos, vestís, **visten.**

PRES. SUBJ. **vista, vistas, vista,** vistamos, vistáis, **vistan.**

IMPF. IND. vestía, etc.; FUT. IND. vestiré, etc.; COND. vestiría, etc.

PRET. IND. vestí, vestiste, **vistió,** vestimos, vestisteis, **vistieron.**

IMPF. SUBJS. **vistiese,** etc.; **vistiera,** etc.; FUT. SUBJ. **vistiere,** etc.

IMPERATIVES **viste,** vestid

IDIOMS

117. *En seguida* ⎫
     Al instante ⎭   At once, immediately

Se lo enviaré a Vd. en seguida (al instante).   I shall send it to you at once.

118. *Tardar en* (+ *infinitive*)   To delay in, be long in

No tardó en llegar.   He was not long in arriving.

119. *A pesar de*   In spite of

Vinieron a pesar de lo que habían dicho.   They came in spite of what they had said.

A

Madrid, 11 de agosto de 19—

Sra. Doña Lucía Holmes,
    Bar Harbor, Maine.

Muy señora mía:

Acabo de recibir la carta de Vd. en la que me dice que no tardará en pasar por Boston en viaje para la costa de Maine. Es muy natural hacer ese viaje en este mes de
5 agosto para ir a donde hace más fresco que en la ciudad

El Museo del Prado, Madrid

RETRATO DE D. BALTASAR CARLOS
(Cuadro de Velázquez)

de Wáshington.   En esa parte de la costa hay panoramas
muy hermosos de las islas y del mar.   Los que vi yo mismo,
hace dos años cuando estuve ahí durante dos meses, me
compensaron completamente el viaje.   Vd., que es artista,
estará pintando ahora esos paisajes de la costa que he visto. 5
Le pido un favor, el de pintarme una.   ¿ Sabe Vd. lo que
haré por Vd.?   Le enviaré en seguida una copia pequeña
de un cuadro famoso de Velázquez.   A mí me parece que
es su mejor retrato ecuestre en cuanto al colorido.   Es el
del príncipe D. Baltasar Carlos a caballo, retrato que se 10
halla aquí en Madrid en el Museo del Prado.

Muchos artistas creen que este Museo del Prado es el
mejor de Europa para los estudiantes, porque contiene más
obras maestras de los pintores famosos que cualquier otro
museo del continente.   No hay sólo pinturas de españoles, 15
las hay también hechas por los italianos Ticiano, Rafael, y
Tintoretto, y por los flamencos Rubens y Van Dyck.
Éstas sirven de modelos a los estudiantes.   De todos
los cuadros de los españoles los que más me gustan son
los de Velázquez.   Hay una gran Sala de Velázquez con 20
más de cuarenta obras suyas.   Todos los días voy allá,
para gozar de ellas, porque soy muy aficionado a la pintura.
Todos los artistas que vienen acá quieren volver a verlas
a menudo.   Por supuesto no dejan de mirar los cuadros
de Goya y de Murillo que están en este museo.   25

La primera vez que fuí al Museo del Prado vi a dos
artistas que estaban copiando el retrato ecuestre de
D. Baltasar Carlos por Velázquez.   Al fin dejaron de pintar,
y el más viejo de los pintores dijo al más joven que quería
vender su pintura.   Éste escuchaba, mientras aquél hablaba 30
del mejor modo de copiar a Velázquez.   Me llegué a ellos, y
no tardé mucho en comprar la pintura.   Se la enviaré a Vd.

Con esperanzas de recibir una carta de Vd., quedo

Su atento y afmo. amigo

Luis Oliver

B

I. *Cuestionario*

1. ¿ A dónde iba a viajar la Sra. Holmes? 2. ¿ Por qué iba a Maine? 3. ¿ Qué hay que ver allí? 4. ¿ Qué favor pidió Luis a la señora? 5. ¿ Qué dijo Luis que enviaría a la señora? 6. ¿ Por qué frecuentan los artistas el Museo del Prado? 7. ¿ Qué pinturas sirven de modelos a los estudiantes? 8. ¿ Qué pintor español le gustaba más a Luis? 9. ¿ Qué copiaban los pintores? 10. ¿ Cómo compró Luis la pintura?

II. *Temas*

1. El viaje de la Sra. Holmes.
2. Los paisajes de la costa de Maine.
3. Los cuadros de la señora.
4. La pintura de Velázquez.
5. El Museo del Prado.
6. Las pinturas de los artistas de otros países.
7. La Sala de Velázquez.
8. Los dos artistas y sus pinturas.
9. La conversación de los artistas.
10. La pintura que compró Luis.

C

Louis. — Please put your hat on at once, Mary, you are always so long in getting ready. You told me yesterday that your mother and you were in favor of going to the theater to-night. I have just bought tickets in order to
5 go to the Royal Theater. It is the one which you like best.[1] We have to pay about twenty pesetas for each ticket in order to enter. This ticket is for you, and that one is for your mother.

Mary. — What good luck! I was about to go out.

---

[1] más.

John is not in favor of going to the theater. He will leave by railroad in the morning for the Escorial, that gloomy old building built by Philip II in the sixteenth century. He will return by El Pardo, a castle built by Charles V in 1543. He is working hard to learn Spanish history. He will stay there for two days. . . Do my mother and I have to put on cloaks? It is not cold in spite of yesterday's rain.

Louis. — It is not necessary to wear cloaks; however, do not fail to carry umbrellas. Where is yours and your mother's? This one is better than that one near you. The ones which are on the table are no good. . . I bought the two for ten pesetas. That one in the corner is for you; this one is for me. Shall we go by taxi or in the street car?

Mary. — We shall go by taxi, of course. . . To-night's play was written by a Spaniard, José Echegaray. Mrs. Mendoza and Captain Martin do not agree in regard to Spanish plays; the former prefers those of Lope de Vega, the latter those of Benavente. You, of course, prefer vaudeville shows or the movies or dances by Gipsy girls.

D

Drill

1. Albert, are you in favor of going to the vaudeville show or to the movies to-night? 2. I like the latter better (**más**) than the former. 3. I do not have to pay more than twenty cents in order to enter. 4. In spite of that, for your sake, I shall go to the vaudeville show to-night. 5. This ticket is for you. 6. John sold it to me two days ago for ten cents. 7. What luck! What you say pleases me very much. 8. Accordingly, I shall have ten cents in order to buy a cigar. 9. I shall not be long in dressing. 10. We shall reach the theater by nine o'clock. 11. We shall stay there for about an hour and a half. 12. Now we are about to go. 13. It is bad weather;

where is my umbrella? 14. This one is yours; I shall
give it to you. 15. This one is older than that one
(*near you*). 16. Those in the corner are my brother's.
17. Shall we go to the theater by taxi? 18. Ask her to
dress (*pres. subj.*) the child as quickly as possible. 19. I
asked them to dress (*imperf. subj.*) the children. 20. They
ask me to serve (*pres. subj.*) them at once. 21. *Captain
Veneno* was written by Alarcón in 1881.

EXERCISE XI

Relative and Interrogative Pronouns, Adjectives, and Adverbs

120. Relative [1] **expressions.** — The table of relatives is
as follows: —

que (invariable)	*who, which, that*	
el cual, los cuales la cual, las cuales el que, los que la que, las que	*who, which*	persons or things
cuyo, cuyos cuya, cuyas	*whose, of which*	
cuanto, cuantos cuanta, cuantas	*all that, all those who, as many (much) as*	
quien, quienes	*who*	persons only
lo cual (invariable) lo que (invariable)	*which* *which, what (that which)*	whole idea
donde (invariable)	*in which (where)*	things only

121. Interrogative [1] **expressions.** — The table of interrogatives is as follows: —

---

[1] Relative and interrogative pronouns referring to persons (not **que**),
when used as direct objects of verbs, require the preposition **a** the same as
nouns. See § **38.** **Conozco a los que hablaron español,** *I know those who
spoke Spanish.* **¿ A quién vió Vd. ?** *Whom did you see?*

¿ qué ?[1] (invariable)	*what ?*	
¿ cuál ? ¿ cuáles ?	*which ? which one ?*	adjectives or pronouns
¿ cuánto ?[1] ¿ cuántos ? ¿ cuánta ? ¿ cuántas ?	*how much ? how many ?*	
¿ quién ? ¿ quiénes ?	*who ?*	pronouns only
¿ de quién ? ¿ de quiénes ?	*of whom ? whose ?*	
¿ dónde ? ¿ cuándo ? ¿ cómo ?	*where ? when ? how ?*	adverbs

(Note that an accent is used to distinguish visually the interrogatives.)

122. Uses of relatives:[2] — 1. **Que** is used more frequently than the other relatives, referring to persons or things, as the subject or object of a verb. (As the object of a preposition **quien** instead of **que** is used for persons.)

El hombre que vino ayer es mi hermano.	The man who came yesterday is my brother.
He visto las cartas que Vd. escribió.	I have seen the letters which you wrote.

2. **Quien** is used for persons, principally after prepositions. Sometimes it includes its antecedent and means *he who*, or is used for *who* after a clause the sense of which is complete.

El estenógrafo de quien Vd. ha hablado acaba de llegar.	The stenographer of whom you have spoken has just arrived.
Quien estudia aprende.	He who studies learns.
He encontrado a mi primo, quien me lo ha dicho.	I have met my cousin, who has told me so.

3. **El cual** and **el que**,[3] since they vary for gender and number, are used instead of **que** or **quien** to avoid ambiguity, particularly when the antecedent and relative are widely

---

[1] Qué and cuánto are used also in exclamations. ¡ Qué bien habla Vd.! *How well you speak !* ¡ Cuánto me alegro ! *How glad I am !*

[2] The relative pronoun is never omitted in Spanish as it frequently is in English. **El periódico que he leído,** *The newspaper (which) I have read.*

[3] For the use of **el que** as a demonstrative pronoun, see § **111.**

separated. They are used also for emphasis, and after prepositions of more than one syllable.

El hijo de la Sra. Navarro, el cual está en la ciudad, vendrá pronto.
Mrs. Navarro's son, who is in town, will come soon.

No he visto hoy al dueño de la casa, el cual es muy simpático.
I have not seen to-day the owner of the house, who is very congenial.

¿ Dónde está la silla sobre la cual puse mi sobretodo?
Where is the chair on which I put my overcoat?

4. **Lo cual** and **lo que** [1] are used to refer to a whole idea, not to a definite noun.

Mi profesor habla despacio, lo cual me gusta.
My professor speaks slowly, which I like.

Leímos lo que han escrito.
We read what they have written.

5. **Cuyo** is a relative adjective, which must directly precede the noun it modifies, and which must agree with it in gender and number.

Preferimos al comerciante cuyos precios son módicos.
We prefer the merchant whose prices are moderate.

Allí está la señora cuyo paraguas hallé.
There is the lady whose umbrella I found.

6. **Cuanto** is used both as a pronoun and as an adjective, and varies for gender and number.

Mi amigo hizo cuanto pudo.
My friend did all that he could.

Cuantos estaban allí murieron.
All those who were there died.

7. **Donde, en donde,** and **a donde,** may be used as relative adverbs.

Éste es el pueblo (en) donde yo vivía.
This is the village in which I used to live.

Pronto veremos la escuela a donde vamos.
We shall soon see the school to which we are going.

---

[1] For the use of **lo que** as a demonstrative pronoun, see § 111.

123. Uses of interrogatives. — Interrogative pronouns, adjectives, and adverbs are used both in direct and in indirect questions.

¿ Qué dijeron los niños?	What did the children say?
¿ Qué cosa es ésta?	What thing is this?
Aquí están varios cuadros.	Here are several pictures.
¿Sabemos cuál comprar?	Do we know which one to buy?
¿ Cuántas manzanas había en el plato?	How many apples were there on the plate?
Sé quiénes son.	I know who they are.
¿ De quién es este abanico?	Whose fan is this?
¿ Dónde, cuándo y cómo murió?	Where, when and how did he die?

VERBS

124. Seguir, *to follow*

PRES. PART. siguiendo; PAST PART. seguido.
PRES. IND. sigo, sigues, sigue, seguimos, seguís, siguen.
PRES. SUBJ. siga, sigas, siga, sigamos, sigáis, sigan.
IMPF. IND. seguía, etc.; FUT. IND. seguiré, etc.; COND. seguiría, etc.
PRET. IND. seguí, seguiste, siguió, seguimos, seguisteis, siguieron.
IMPF. SUBJS. siguiese, etc.; siguiera, etc.; FUT. SUBJ. siguiere, etc.
IMPERATIVES sigue, seguid.

125. Morir, *to die*

PRES. PART. muriendo; PAST PART. muerto.
PRES. IND. muero, mueres, muere, morimos, morís, mueren.
PRES. SUBJ. muera, mueras, muera, muramos, muráis, mueran.
IMPF. IND. moría, etc.; FUT. IND. moriré, etc.; COND. moriría, etc.
PRET. IND. morí, moriste, murió, morimos, moristeis, murieron.
IMPF. SUBJS. muriese, etc.; muriera, etc.; FUT. SUBJ. muriere, etc.
IMPERATIVES muere, morid.

126. **Conocer,** *to know*

PRES. PART. conociendo; PAST PART. conocido.

PRES. IND. **conozco,** conoces, conoce, conocemos, conocéis, conocen.

PRES. SUBJ. **conozca, conozcas, conozca, conozcamos, conozcáis, conozcan.**

IMPF. IND. conocía, etc.; FUT. IND. conoceré, etc.; COND. conocería, etc.

PRET. IND. conocí, conociste, conoció, conocimos, conocisteis, conocieron.

IMPF. SUBJS. conociese, etc.; conociera, etc.; FUT. SUBJ. conociere, etc.

IMPERATIVES conoce, conoced.

IDIOMS

127. *Echar de menos* To miss, feel the lack of

Echamos de menos los gozos del campo. We miss the pleasures of the country.

128. *Dar con* To happen upon, meet

Di con ellos esta mañana. I happened upon (met) them this morning.

129. *Mientras tanto* *Entretanto* Meanwhile

Mientras tanto (entretanto) hablábamos de la corrida.
Meanwhile we were talking of the bull fight.

A

Madrid, 16 de agosto de 19 —.

Querido amigo mío:

«¡A los toros! ¡Vamos a los toros! ¿Quién va a torear?» Poco después de oír esos gritos di con Carlos, y nos decidimos a ir a la Plaza de Toros. Pronto vimos a
5 un hombre a caballo, vestido de colores vistosos, a quien seguían muchos jóvenes entusiastas. — ¿Quién es aquel

En la Plaza de Toros, Madrid

hombre? ¿Qué hace? — ¡Vaya! ¿No sabe Vd. quién es? Es un torero muy conocido. Le conozco bien. Es del pueblo en donde vivía yo cuando era niño. ¡Cuántas veces le he visto torear! — Entonces Carlos y yo hicimos cuanto pudimos por acercarnos al torero, lo que deseaba yo viva- 5 mente, pero no lo logramos.

¿Cómo puedo pintar una corrida? Doce mil aficionados en la Plaza de Toros esperando la lidia, todos hablando o agitando abanicos de muchos colores. Mientras tanto los músicos tocan con frenesí. Sale al redondel la cuadrilla de 10 todos los lidiadores con vestidos de muchos colores, bordados de oro y plata. El presidente de la Plaza desde su palco le echa al alguacil mayor la llave del toril. Se van del redondel los que no tienen nada que hacer al principio del combate. Sigue un silencio súbito. El toril se abre, y 15 sale el toro, cuyo nombre, color y casta ya saben todos. Oye los gritos del pueblo. Mira alrededor y ve a los picadores a caballo. Éstos deben ser sus enemigos, y se arroja contra uno de ellos, de cuya garrocha recibe un fuerte aguijonazo. Vuelve al ataque. Por fin quedan dos caballos 20 muertos y un picador herido.

Viene ahora una suerte bonita, la de los banderilleros. Vi a uno de éstos que esperaba el ataque del animal, agitando las banderillas delante de él. Acometió el toro al hombre, y éste saltó diestramente a un lado y le clavó en el cuello 25 las lanzas pequeñas o banderillas cubiertas de papeles de varios colores. Con sus capas los capeadores atrajeron el toro a otra parte del redondel y se repitió la misma suerte varias veces, hasta que seis banderillas le colgaban del cuello. 30

Al fin vino el matador. Era el que habíamos visto en la calle, y de quien mi amigo me había contado la vida. Con la muleta encarnada, le dió varios pases al toro, y al cabo la estocada final, que le hizo caer muriendo al suelo. El aplauso del pueblo fué pasmoso. Llegaron las mulas rica- 35 mente engalanadas, y arrastraron los caballos muertos y el toro. Cubrieron las manchas de sangre con arena, lo cual me hizo pensar en la novela de Blasco Ibáñez: *Sangre y Arena*. Sucedió lo mismo, poco más o menos, con otros cinco toros, y se acabó la corrida.

5 Si viene Vd. alguna vez a España, debe ir a una corrida. Quedo como siempre

Su afmo. amigo
LUIS

B

I. *Cuestionario*

1. ¿ Qué gritaron en las calles ? 2. ¿ A quién vieron a caballo ? 3. ¿ Por qué conocía Carlos bien al torero ? 4. ¿ Que hacía el pueblo en la Plaza de Toros ? 5. ¿ Qué hizo la cuadrilla antes de la salida del toro ? 6. ¿ A quién atacó primero el toro ? 7. ¿ Qué suerte bonita siguió a la de los picadores ? 8. ¿ No hicieron nada los capeadores ? 9. ¿ Cómo murió el toro ? 10. ¿ Qué se hizo después de arrastrar los animales muertos ?

II. *Temas*

1. Los gritos en las calles.	6. Los picadores atacados.
2. El torero muy conocido.	7. Los banderilleros y la
3. El pueblo en la Plaza de Toros.	suerte de banderillas.
4. La llegada de la cuadrilla.	8. Los capeadores.
5. El toro sale.	9. Al fin, el matador.
	10. El toro muerto.

C

LOUIS. — John, you were telling me a week ago how much you miss football games here in Spain. Instead of a football game, I was present this afternoon, with Lieutenant González, at a bullfight, which was very interesting.

5 JOHN. — What is this ? What do you mean ? What bull-

fight? When did you go? When and where did you buy
the tickets? What have you there in your hand?
Whose bright-colored fan is that? From whom did you
get it?

Louis. — How many questions at once! I shall do 5
whatever I can[1] in order to tell you what you want to
know. I was going along the street of Alcalá, following a
man on horseback, dressed in bright colors, when I happened upon Lieutenant González, with whom I exchange
English lessons for Spanish lessons. . . — " Who is that 10
man on horseback? " I asked him. — " Do you not know
who he is? " said he. " He is a bullfighter. Do you wish
to go to the bullfight with me, this afternoon? " — " What
a question! " said I. " Let us go at once." The bullfight was as interesting as a football game. . . Where did 15
you go, meanwhile, and with whom?

John. — I was going with Mary to the church of Saint
Francis the Great, when we happened upon Charles Williams.
He is the man of whom I was talking with you last week,
who is studying fine arts, and whose sister is Mary's friend. 20
Charles, and his mother, who knows Madrid well, are
helping us study Spanish history. I am well satisfied with
what I have done to-day. " He who studies well, learns."

Louis. — I have never seen such a man! Who would
like an old building better than a bullfight? As for me, 25
Lieutenant González explained to me all that happened
this afternoon, and now I know exactly what a bullfight is.

D

Drill

1. Tell me, Albert, where are you going so fast, and
with whom? 2. I am going to the football game with
these men who are following me. 3. I do not believe

---

[1] Present subjunctive (§ 150, 1, footnote 5).

that you know (*pres. subj.*) them. 4. How many of
them do you know? 5. I know those who (**los que**)
wear red caps, and the tall one who comes from time to
time to my Spanish class. 6. Is he the student whose
father died last week? 7. I do not believe that his father
has died (*pres. perf. subj.*). 8. It is his uncle who was dying.
9. His father and mine used to know each other several
years ago. 10. Whose tickets are those which you have
in your hand? 11. Which one is for me? 12. You
know the proverb, "He who asks, receives." 13. I do
not know what you mean. 14. These tickets are for some
friends (*f.*) of my sister, whom I happened upon this
morning. 15. They do not live here now, and accordingly
they miss the football games very much. 16. What good
luck! When will you introduce me to them? 17. What
you ask is impossible. 18. I cannot help laughing at you.
19. Goodbye, I do not want you to follow (*pres. subj.*) me.
20. The more you ask from me, the less I shall do for
you. 21. I am acquainted with the life of Cervantes,
which is very interesting. 22. Who is following us?
23. Meanwhile, all those who were there died.

EXERCISE XII

Reflexive Verbs — *Mismo* — Passive Voice

130. Reflexive verbs are conjugated like the following
model: —

Levantarse, *to rise, get up*

PRESENT INDICATIVE	PRESENT PERFECT INDICATIVE
yo me levanto	yo me he levantado
tú te levantas	tú te has levantado
él, ella, Vd. se levanta	él, ella, Vd. se ha levantado
nosotros nos levantamos	nosotros nos hemos levantado
vosotros os levantáis	vosotros os habéis levantado
ellos, ellas, Vds. se levantan	ellos, ellas, Vds. se han levantado

IMPF. IND., yo me levantaba, etc.

PRET. IND., yo me levanté, etc.

FUT. IND., yo me levantaré, etc.

COND. IND., yo me levantaría etc.

PRESENT PARTICIPLE, levantándose

PRES. SUBJ., yo me levante, etc.

-se IMPF. SUBJ., yo me levantase, etc.

-ra IMPF. SUBJ., yo me levantara, etc.

FUT. SUBJ., yo me levantare, etc.

IMPERATIVE CONSTRUCTIONS

Familiar Speech		*Formal Speech*	
SINGULAR	PLURAL	SINGULAR	PLURAL
IMPERATIVE		SUBJUNCTIVE	
levántate	levantaos	levántese Vd.	levántense Vds.
SUBJUNCTIVE		levantémonos	
no te levantes	no os levantéis	no se levante Vd	no se levanten Vds.

131. Equivalents of English constructions. — The reflexive verbs are used in Spanish as the equivalents of the following English constructions: —

1. *Reflexive verbs.* (Spanish like English.)

Me lavo ahora.　　　　I am washing myself now.

Se expusieron al peligro.　They exposed themselves to the danger.

2. *Reciprocal verbs.* (Spanish like English.)

Nos escribiremos cada semana.　We shall write to each other every week.

Se culpan (los unos a los otros).[1]　They blame one another.

3. *Simple (non-reflexive) verbs* [2] (in English).

Los soldados se atreven a ir.　The soldiers dare to go.

Me quejé de lo que habían hecho.　I complained of what they had done.

4. *Passive voice* (in English).

Eso no puede hacerse.　That cannot be done.

El español se habla aquí.[3]　Spanish is spoken here.

---

[1] If necessary for the sake of clearness, **el uno al otro,** etc., may be added.

[2] Some simple verbs acquire a new meaning when used reflexively. **Ir,** *to go,* **irse,** *to go away;* **dormir,** *to sleep,* **dormirse,** *to fall asleep;* **acostar,** *to put to bed,* **acostarse,** *to go to bed.*

[3] BUT: **Aquí se habla español** (*without the article*).

(a) The English impersonal construction is expressed by the reflexive in Spanish.

Se dice que habrá poca nieve.	It is said that there will be little snow.
Se cree que vendrán.	It is believed that they will come.
Se me figura que es verdad.	It seems to me that it is true.

(b) If the subject of a verb in the passive (*in English*) refers to a definite person or persons, it may be expressed as the direct or indirect object of a reflexive verb (in singular only) in Spanish.

Se ve a los niños.	The children are seen. (One sees the children.)
Se les ve distintamente.	They are seen distinctly. (One sees them distinctly.)
Se me dice.	I am told.

132. Mismo, -a, -os, -as, *self*, is used to emphasize the subject or object of a verb.

Yo mismo lo dije a Carlos.	I myself told it to Charles.
Lo dieron a María misma.[1]	They gave it to Mary herself.

133. The Spanish passive voice (*Infrequently used*). — The passive voice in Spanish is formed by the verb ser [2] followed by the past participle, which agrees in gender and number with the subject.

> **Este libro fué escrito por [3] Pérez Galdós.**
> This book was written by Pérez Galdós.
>
> **Somos respetados de [3] nuestros amigos.**
> We are respected by our friends.

---

[1] When **mismo** means *same*, it precedes the noun. **Estamos estudiando en la misma universidad,** *We are studying in the same university.*

[2] For the use of **estar** with past participles, see § **14,** 4.

[3] *By* is usually expressed by **por** in the passive construction, but **de** may be used after some verbs which denote mental action.

VERBS

134. Acostarse, *to go to bed*

PRES. PART. acostándose; PAST PART. acostado.

PRES. IND. me acuesto, te acuestas, se acuesta, nos acostamos, os acostáis, se acuestan.

PRES. SUBJ. me acueste, te acuestes, se acueste, nos acostemos, os acostéis, se acuesten.

IMPF. IND. me acostaba, etc.; FUT. IND. me acostaré, etc.; COND. me acostaría, etc.

PRET. IND. me acosté, te acostaste, se acostó, nos acostamos, os acostasteis, se acostaron.

IMPF. SUBJS. me acostase, etc.; me acostara, etc.; FUT. SUBJ. me acostare, etc.

IMPERATIVES acuéstate, acostaos.

135. Conducir, *to conduct*

PRES. PART. conduciendo; PAST PART. conducido.

PRES. IND. conduzco, conduces, conduce, conducimos, conducís, conducen.

PRES. SUBJ. conduzca, conduzcas, conduzca, conduzcamos, conduzcáis, conduzcan.

IMPF. IND. conducía, etc.; FUT. IND. conduciré, etc.; COND. conduciría, etc.

PRET. IND. conduje, condujiste, condujo, condujimos, condujisteis, condujeron.

IMPF. SUBJS. condujese, etc.; condujera, etc.; FUT. SUBJ. condujere, etc.

IMPERATIVES conduce, conducid.

136. Jugar, *to play*

PRES. PART. jugando; PAST PART. jugado.

PRES. IND. juego, juegas, juega, jugamos, jugáis, juegan.

PRES. SUBJ. juegue, juegues, juegue, juguemos, juguéis, jueguen.

IMPF. IND. jugaba, etc.; FUT. IND. jugaré, etc.; COND. jugaría, etc.

PRET. IND. **jugué,** jugaste, jugó, jugamos, jugasteis, jugaron.
IMPF. SUBJS. jugase, etc.; jugara, etc.; FUT. SUBJ. jugare, etc.
IMPERATIVES **juega,** jugad.

IDIOMS

137. *Tratarse de* To be a question of, deal with

Se trata del gobierno del país. It is a question of the government of the country.

138. *Prestar atención a* To pay attention to

Preste Vd. atención cuando hablo. Pay attention when I talk.

139. *De buena (mala) gana* Willingly (unwillingly), gladly

Volvimos de buena gana a la ciudad. We returned willingly to the city.

A

Toledo, 22 de agosto de 19—.

Querido amigo:

Me hallo ahora en Toledo, antigua capital de España.
No pude menos de contemplar esta ciudad con emoción al
acercarme a ella. Me acordé de la vida del Cid, gran héroe
5 nacional de los castellanos, y cómo entró en la ciudad con
su rey, al rendirse los moros a fines del siglo once. Quien
mira la ciudad puede fácilmente imaginarse combates
épicos bajo sus murallas.

Anoche, cuando me acosté, me decidí a levantarme
10 temprano porque quería salir a pasearme cuando hacía
fresco. Por lo tanto, me levanté temprano esta mañana,
me lavé, me vestí y salí. En una calle estrecha di con tres
mujeres que caminaban despacio hacia el mercado y hablaban de sus maridos. No me prestaban atención a mí, y
15 ocupaban toda la calle. Una de ellas se quejaba de lo que
hacía su marido, diciendo que se divertía fuera de casa,

TOLEDO, ANTIGUA CAPITAL DE ESPAÑA

MIGUEL DE CERVANTES SAAVEDRA

jugaba a la pelota, no cuidaba de la familia, y que ella no era respetada de sus amigas a causa de él. La segunda mujer dijo que el suyo se quejaba de achaques imaginarios, se acostaba temprano y se levantaba tarde, y que no cuidaba tampoco de la familia. La tercera dijo. . . pero de buena 5 gana me escapé de todo aquello, y entré en una librería cuya puerta acababa de abrirse.

— Vi abierta la puerta —le dije al dependiente—y quiero saber si se venden aquí buenas ediciones de los autores clásicos. Se me mostró ayer la casa en donde vivía Cer- 10 vantes mientras estuvo en Toledo. Creo que Vd. debe de tener buenas ediciones de sus obras. — Sí, señor, mire Vd. las ediciones del *Quijote.* Ésta tiene muchos lindos grabados, pero ésa es más gruesa. ¿ Cuál desea Vd. ? — Se trata de saber cuál sería mejor para mi biblioteca. — ¿ No 15 desea Vd. las dos ? — ¿ Cuánto valen ? — Se las pondré a sesenta pesetas, caballero. — ¡ Caramba ! ¡ Qué precio tan subido ! — Pues, estas ediciones nunca son baratas, y valen mucho más de lo que pido. Sin embargo, si Vd. desea las dos, puedo vendérselas por cincuenta pesetas. — Bueno, me 20 las llevo. — Espero enseñárselas a mis amigos al llegar yo a los Estados Unidos.

Con muchos recuerdos a todos los amigos, soy siempre

Su afmo. amigo
Luis

B

I. *Cuestionario*

1. ¿ En qué ciudad se hallaba Luis ?   2. ¿ De qué se acordó ?   3. ¿ Por qué quería levantarse temprano ? 4. ¿ Qué hizo antes de salir por la mañana ?   5. ¿ Con quiénes dió en la calle ?   6. ¿ De quiénes hablaban ellas ?   7. ¿ Qué hacían los maridos ?   8. ¿ En donde entró Luis ?   9. ¿ Qué libros buscaba ?   10. ¿ Qué compró al fin, y cuánto pagó ?

II. *Temas*

1. Toledo, el Cid y los moros.
2. La salida de Luis por la mañana.
3. Las tres mujeres que vió en la calle.
4. Las quejas de la primera mujer.
5. Las quejas de la segunda.
6. La librería con la puerta abierta.
7. La casa de Cervantes.
8. Los libros que buscaba Luis.
9. Las dos ediciones del *Quijote*.
10. Cómo compró Luis las dos.

C

LOUIS (*to John who had just lain down*). — Get up at once, John, and put on your coat. Hurry up! Oh, excuse me, hadn't you waked up yet? . . . While you are washing your face and shaving, I shall tell you what I did yesterday.
5 It deals with a trip that I made with Charles Williams to the most interesting city in Spain. At least that is what I think.

JOHN. — I shall get up willingly. . . You mean Toledo, do you not? Toledo, that wonderful city which used to
10 be called "Spanish Rome," and whose name is found so frequently in all books in which the history of Spain is treated. Did you go through its winding streets, and sit down on the bank of the river Tagus? Did you imagine yourself to be in the year 1085, entering through the great
15 gate with King Alphonso VI and the Cid?

LOUIS. — I did not imagine any of that; it was too hot. We gladly took a walk along the bank of the Tagus in order to cool off. While we were walking, talking to each other, we approached a bathing-place where suits were
20 rented. We decided to swim in that river on whose banks grains of gold used to be found. At least, that is what is told. We did not find gold, but exceedingly many sand-flies. In order to escape them, I threw myself quickly into

the water, without paying attention to the rocks. I struck against a rock and hurt my head.

JOHN. — Why do you complain of such an insignificant thing? . . . Were you shown the house in which Cervantes used to live? Did you sit down in the inn where he used 5 to eat?

LOUIS. — I haven't time to tell you all that. I have to bathe my head.

D

Drill

1. Why did Albert and you get up so early this morning? 2. You washed your faces and hands and dressed at a quarter after five. 3. You talked to each other from time to time. 4. I paid no attention to what you were saying. 5. I did not dare complain of the noise. 6. I remembered that you (*pl.*) had gone to bed late. 7. However, I fell asleep willingly when the door closed. 8. It is said that you often play pelota to amuse yourselves. 9. I cannot help telling you so. 10. You were seen. 11. Postcards are sold in the tobacco-stores. 12. They were sold to you last week. 13. I played pelota day before yesterday.

EXERCISE XIII

The Subjunctive (I) — Sequence of Tenses

140. Use of the subjunctive: In noun clauses.[1] — The subjunctive mood is used in a subordinate clause when there is uncertainty in the mind of the speaker. The indicative, on the contrary, implies certainty in the mind of the speaker. The subjunctive is used in Spanish in many instances where English uses the infinitive or the indicative. The subjunctive is used in noun clauses,[2] when the subject

---

[1] A noun clause is one used as the subject or object of a verb.

[2] The conjunction **que**, *that*, is used to introduce both subjunctive and indicative clauses.

of the dependent clause is different from that of the principal clause,[1] after: (1) volitional verbs; (2) emotional verbs; (3) verbs of doubt, denial, and interrogation; and (4) impersonal expressions not indicating certainty.

1. After volitional verbs (command,[2] desire, permission, prohibition, preference, advice, etc.).

Me manda que escriba la lección.	He orders me to write the lesson.
Quiero que Vd. me traiga un vaso de agua.	I want you to bring me a glass of water.
Permitió que fuésemos con ellos.	He permitted us to go with them.

2. After emotional verbs (joy, sorrow, fear, hope,[3] surprise, etc.).

Me alegro (de) que Vds. hayan venido.	I am glad that you have come.
Siento que ella se vaya tan pronto.	I am sorry that she is going away so soon.
Temieron que lo hiciésemos.	They feared that we would do it.

3. After verbs of doubt, denial, and interrogation (implying doubt).

Dudo que lo hagan.	I doubt that they will do it.
¿ Cree Vd. que vengan pasado mañana ?	Do you believe that they will come day after to-morrow ?
No creo que vengan.	I do not believe that they will come.

(a) Verbs of doubt, in the negative, and verbs of belief, in the affirmative, take the indicative.

---

[1] When the subject of two consecutive verbs is the same, the second verb is in the infinitive. **Temo no llegar a tiempo,** *I am afraid that I shall not arrive in time.*

[2] **Decir** and **escribir** require the subjunctive when they express a command, and the indicative when they make a statement. **Dígale Vd. que vaya,** *Tell him to go.* BUT: **Me dijo que iría,** *He told me that he would go.*

[3] When certainty is implied, the indicative is used with **esperar.**

No dudo que me hablarán.	I do not doubt that they will speak to me.
Creo que llegarán a tiempo.	I believe that they will arrive in time.

(b) The indicative is used after questions, in case there is no doubt in the mind of the speaker concerning the reality of the statement in the dependent clause.

¿ No sabe Vd. que está malo ?	Don't you know that he is ill ? (*He really is ill.*)
¿ No cree Vd. que soy feliz ?	Don't you believe that I am happy ? (*I really am happy.*)

4. After impersonal expressions not indicating certainty.

Es preciso que lo hallemos.	It is necessary for us to find it.
Era posible que abriese la puerta.	It was possible that he would open the door.
BUT: Es cierto que vinieron.	It is certain that they came.

(a) Impersonal verbs are followed by the infinitive, in case the dependent verb in English does not have a subject expressed, or when the expressed subject is not emphatic.

Es preciso ir temprano.	It is necessary to go early.
Le es preciso ir temprano.	It is necessary for him to go early.
BUT: Es preciso que vaya él temprano.	It is necessary for *him* to go early. (*He* must go early.)

141. Use of the future subjunctive. — The future subjunctive, which denotes an indefinite condition or hypothesis, may express either present or future time. It is rarely used now in spoken Spanish, except in proverbs, axioms, etc., as the present subjunctive has largely replaced it.

Lo que te dijere el espejo, no te lo dirán en consejo.	What your mirror might tell you, your close friends will not say to you.
Sea lo que fuere, no me importa.	Let it be what it may, it does not matter to me.

VERBS

142.   Caer, *to fall*

Pres. Part. **cayendo;** Past Part. **caído.**
Pres. Ind. **caigo,** caes, cae, caemos, caéis, caen.
Pres. Subj. **caiga, caigas, caiga, caigamos, caigáis, caigan.**
Impf. Ind. caía, etc.; Fut. Ind. caeré, etc.; Cond. caería, etc.
Pret. Ind. caí, caíste, **cayó,** caímos, caísteis, **cayeron.**
Impf. Subjs. cayese, etc.; **cayera,** etc.; Fut. Subj. **cayere,** etc.
Imperatives cae, caed.

143.   Oír, *to hear*

Pres. Part. **oyendo;** Past Part. oído.
Pres. Ind. **oigo, oyes, oye,** oímos, oís, **oyen.**
Pres. Subj. **oiga, oigas, oiga, oigamos, oigáis, oigan.**
Impf. Ind. oía, etc.; Fut. Ind. oiré, etc.; Cond. oiría, etc
Pret. Ind. oí, oíste, **oyó,** oímos, oísteis, **oyeron.**
Impf. Subjs. **oyese,** etc.; **oyera,** etc.; Fut. Subj. **oyere,** etc.
Imperatives **oye,** oíd.

144.   Valer, *to be worth*

Pres. Part. valiendo; Past Part. valido.
Pres. Ind. **valgo,** vales, vale, valemos, valéis, valen.
Pres. Subj. **valga, valgas, valga, valgamos, valgáis, valgan.**
Impf. Ind. valía, etc.; Fut. Ind. **valdré,** etc.; Cond. **valdría,**
etc.
Pret. Ind. valí, valiste, valió, valimos, valisteis, valieron.
Impf. Subjs. valiese, etc.; valiera, etc.; Fut. Subj. valiere, etc.
Imperatives vale, valed.

IDIOMS

145. *Hacer falta a (uno)*   To be lacking, be in want of
Me hace falta el tiempo.   I lack the time.

146. *Valer la pena*   To be worth while
No vale la pena leerlo.   It is not worth while to read it.

147. *De antemano*   In advance, beforehand
Obtuve un permiso de antemano.   I obtained a permit in advance.

148. Reference Table for Sequence of Tenses

Verb of the principal clause	Verb of the dependent clause [1]	Time of action of the dependent clause compared to that of the principal clause
1. Pres. Ind. 2. Fut. Ind.	Pres. Subj. Impf. Subj. Pres. Perf. Subj.	Same *or* following Prior (*simple tense*) Prior (*compound tense*)
3. Imperative 4. Pres. Subj. (*used as imperative*)	Pres. Subj.	Following
5. Impf. Ind. 6. Pret. Ind. 7. Cond. Ind.	Impf. Subj. Pluperf. Subj.	Same *or* following Prior (*compound tense*)
8 Pres. Perf. Ind.	Pres. Subj. Impf. Subj.	Following Same

1.
No creo que vengan ahora. (*Same*)	I do not believe that they are coming now.
Dudo que vengan mañana. (*Following*)	I doubt that they will come to-morrow.
Temo que no lo hiciese (hiciera) bien. (*Prior, simple tense*)	I fear that he did not do it well.
Es posible que haya salido. (*Prior, compound tense*)	It is possible that he has gone out.

2.
Mañana le permitiré que trabaje conmigo. (*Same*)	To-morrow I shall permit him to work with me.
Le mandaré que los compre. (*Following*)	I shall order him to buy (that he buy) them.
Vd. se alegrará de que yo lo hiciese (hiciera). (*Prior, simple tense*)	You will be glad that I did it.
Vd. sentirá que esto haya sucedido. (*Prior, compound tense*)	You will be sorry that this has happened.

---

[1] Simple tenses in the dependent clause in English are regularly expressed by simple tenses in Spanish, and compound tenses by compound tenses in Spanish.

3. **Escríbele que me envíe aquellos libros.** (*Following*)

Write to him to send me those books.

4. **Permítame Vd. que lea este periódico.** (*Following*)

Allow me to read this newspaper.

5.
- **Dudábamos que trabajasen (trabajaran).** (*Same*)

  We doubted that they were working.
- **Mi hermano me pedía que le ayudase (ayudara).** (*Following*)

  My brother used to ask me to help (that I should help) him.
- **Sentíamos que no hubiesen (hubieran) escrito.** (*Prior, compound tense*)

  We were sorry that they had not written.

6.
- **Pedí a Jorge que me acompañase (acompañara).** (*Following*)

  I asked George to accompany me.
- **Temieron que yo no hubiese (hubiera) comprado los billetes.** (*Prior, compound tense*)

  They feared that I had not bought the tickets.

7.
- **Si estuvieran aquí ahora temería que lo hiciesen (hicieran).** (*Same*)

  If they were here now I should fear that they would do it.
- **Le pediría que viniese (viniera).** (*Following*)

  I should ask him to come.
- **Dudaría que hubiesen (hubieran) llegado.** (*Prior*)

  I should doubt that they had arrived.

8.
- **Me han pedido que les escriba.** (*Following*)

  They have asked me to write to them.
- **He dudado que lo hiciesen (hicieran).** (*Same*)

  I have doubted that they were doing it.

A

Madrid, 27 de agosto de 19—.

Querido amigo:

Me alegro de que hayan llegado varias cartas hoy de los Estados Unidos, entre las cuales di con la de Vd. Es lástima que no vengan cartas más a menudo. Todavía me

LA BIBLIOTECA DEL ESCORIAL

hacen falta los periódicos que le pedí que me enviase. Los echo de menos.

Mi amigo Carlos vino a verme hace unos días, y quiso que fuésemos al Escorial, ciudad pequeña al noroeste de Madrid, en la cual está el real monasterio de San Lorenzo, .5 que fué edificado por Felipe II. Este monasterio contiene el Panteón de los Reyes de España, una iglesia, un convento, y una biblioteca de importancia. Carlos temía que me fuese de España sin ver el Escorial, y por eso, deseaba que ayer le acompañase allá. 10

Cuando vino Carlos ayer, estaba yo listo para salir. Era preciso que volviésemos a Madrid el mismo día, y por lo tanto no valía la pena comprar billetes dos veces, y pedimos en la estación que se nos vendiesen billetes de ida y vuelta. Yo dudaba que entrásemos en el Escorial sin obtener per- 15 miso especial de antemano, y no creía que se nos permitiese entrar por la mañana. A pesar de mis dudas, cuando nos presentamos a la puerta de entrada, estaba abierta, y pasamos en seguida al patio que conduce a la iglesia.

La iglesia es muy grande y hay unas cincuenta capillas 20 laterales. Queríamos que se nos permitiese entrar en el oratorio donde murió Felipe II, y en el Panteón de los Reyes. Un fraile, que nos oyó hablar, nos condujo allá, donde vimos las tumbas de más de veinte reyes y reinas. No tardamos mucho en subir a la biblioteca en donde vimos 25 muchos manuscritos muy antiguos.

Al llegar a Madrid, dije a Carlos: — Me alegro de que Vd. me haya acompañado hoy. Me marcho de Madrid muy pronto. — ¿ Es posible que Vd. se vaya tan pronto ? Espero que vuelva a vernos antes de salir de España. — 30 Dudo que sea posible, porque tendré que pasar por Valencia a Barcelona, donde me embarcaré para América. Nos despedimos con muchas promesas de escribirnos a menudo.

Siempre su afmo. amigo

Luis

B

I. *Cuestionario*

1. ¿ De qué se alegró Luis ? 2. ¿ Había recibido los periódicos tan deseados ? 3. ¿ A dónde quiso Carlos que fuesen ? 4. ¿ Qué contiene el monasterio del Escorial ? 5. ¿ Qué temía Carlos ? 6. ¿ Qué pidieron que se les vendiese en la estación ? 7. ¿ Creía Luis que se les permitiese entrar en el monasterio ? 8. ¿ Qué hizo el fraile que los oyó hablar ? 9. ¿ Por qué se alegró Luis de que Carlos le hubiese acompañado ? 10. ¿ Volverían a verse pronto los dos amigos ?

II. *Temas*

1. La llegada de las cartas.
2. El deseo de Carlos de hacer un viaje con Luis.
3. Lo que hay en el monasterio de San Lorenzo.
4. Los billetes de ida y vuelta.
5. La probabilidad de poder entrar en el Escorial.
6. Las capillas y el panteón de la iglesia.
7. El fraile amigo.
8. La alegría de Luis y la tristeza de Carlos.
9. El viaje de Luis por España.
10. La vuelta a los Estados Unidos.

C

(Use the subjunctive, whenever possible, instead of the infinitive)

MARY. — Listen [1], Louis, it is impossible for you to go with John and me to the Escorial to-day, isn't it ? It will be necessary for you to go with Captain Martin to the Central Pelota Court in order to play pelota. I am sorry
5 that you are not able to go with us. My mother told [2] me to ask [2] you to go. I am afraid that she is ill, and accordingly it is necessary for John and me to go without her. I am glad that I obtained,[3] in advance, her permission to go.

---

[1] oír.   [2] Volitional use.   [3] haber obtenido.

Louis. — It is a pity that you (*pl.*) have to go without me. It isn't worth while, however, to ask me to go. It is not possible for me to have a good time when I am with John and you, because you are talking to each other all the time. Why did your mother wish me to go with you? //5

Mary. — Well, John has wanted me to go to the Escorial with him for several days. He wished us to go by automobile, but my mother was afraid that we would have an accident. She doubts that we shall be able to find good roads, and she does not think that John knows how to 10 drive well.

Louis. — It is very probable that John will ruin the automobile. Permit me to tell[1] you, nevertheless, that I am not going. I want to play pelota. . . It is very interesting. It is played like handball, but the court is very 15 large, and the players have a gourd-shaped basket fastened to their right hands to catch and throw the ball. Most men lack sufficient strength to play well.

Mary. — I do not believe that I like that game. Good-bye, it is necessary that John and I leave at once. I do 20 not want John to go too fast.

D

(Practise, also, the sentences below the table in § **148**.)

1. I am glad that you are going to the city to-morrow morning.   2. It was necessary for me to go as soon as possible.   3. I doubt that you can get up early enough. 4. Did you want us to go with you?   5. I do not believe that you were at the station, the other time, when the employee called " All aboard."   6. Listen, John, Albert wanted you to buy for him a ticket to the movies.   7. He asked me to buy it yesterday.   8. I was afraid that he did not have enough money to pay me.   9. Do you not know that he is rich?   10. I do not believe that the

---

[1] Merely a statement.

ticket is worth five pesetas; it is worth only two pesetas.
11. It will not be worth while for us to buy tickets in
advance.   12. I was hoping that you had received a check
for fifty dollars from your father.   13. Did you not tell
him to send it to you?   14. It is probable that I shall
receive it this afternoon.   15. I am sorry that it did not
come yesterday.   16. I am afraid that you (*pl.*) will fall.
17. He heard them when they fell.   18. We lack the
money; do you hear what I am saying?

EXERCISE XIV

The Subjunctive (II)

149. In adjective clauses.[1] — The subjunctive is used in
adjective clauses whenever indefiniteness or uncertainty is
expressed or implied in either the principal clause or in the
dependent relative clause.

¿ Hay persona cualquiera que pueda saber toda la historia ?	Is there any person who can know the whole story ?
Quienquiera que sea, no le escucharé.	Whoever he may be, I shall not listen to him.
No hay nadie que pueda probarlo.	There is no one who can prove it.
Busco un joven[2] que hable español.	I am looking for a young man (*indefinite*) who speaks Spanish.
BUT: Conozco a un joven que habla español.	I know a young man (*definite*) who speaks Spanish.

150. In adverbial clauses.[3] — 1. In clauses which express
indefinite future time,[4] after:[5]

---

[1] An adjective clause is one introduced by a relative pronoun.

[2] The preposition **a** is not required in this case, since the direct object
is not a *definite* personal noun. See § **38**.

[3] An adverbial clause is one introduced by an adverb or by a conjunctive expression.

[4] Future time considered from the standpoint of the verb of the principal clause.

[5] The subjunctive is also used to express indefinite place, manner, and

cuando, *when*	luego que
antes (de) que, *before*	así que } *as soon as*
después (de) que, *after*	mientras (que), *while, as long as*
hasta que, *until*	siempre que, *whenever*

Cuando vengan, iremos al teatro.
When they come, we shall go to the theater.

Dijo que vendría luego que se fuese su padre.
He said that he would come as soon as his father went away.

Prometió guardarlo hasta que yo viese a mis amigos.
He promised to keep it until I should see my friends.

2. In purpose and result clauses, after such expressions as:

para que } *in order that,*	de manera que } *so that,*
a fin de que } *so that*	de modo que } *so as*

Me envió dinero para que comprase vestidos.
He sent me money in order that (so that) I should buy clothes.

Escriban Vds. el ejercicio de modo que (de manera que) yo pueda leerlo.
Write the exercise so that I can read it.

3. In clauses of concession and restriction, after such expressions as:

aunque,[1] *although*	en caso (de) que, *in case (that)*
a pesar de que, *in spite of*	con tal que, *provided (that)*
por (*adjective or adverb*) que, *however*	a menos que, *unless*
dado que, *granted that*	sin que, *without*

Aunque venga, no nos lo enseñará.
Although he may come, he will not show it to us.

Por fuerte que sea, no puede levantar este peso.
However strong he may be, he cannot raise this weight.

Se lo daré, con tal de que me trate bien.
I shall give it to him, provided he treats me well.

---

amount. **Iré a donde vayan los otros,** *I shall go wherever the others go.*
Llevaré cuanto ponga Vd. en la maleta, *I shall take whatever you may put into the suitcase.*

[1] **Aunque** is followed by the indicative when it states an accomplished fact. **Aunque vino anoche, no le vi,** *Although he came last night, I did not see him.*

151. In conditional sentences. — In less vivid future conditions,[1] and in conditions contrary to fact in present time, the clause containing the condition (*protasis*) is usually introduced by **si,** and the verb is in the imperfect subjunctive (*either* **-se** *or* **-ra**); in the clause stating the conclusion (*apodosis*), the verb is in the conditional or the **-ra** imperfect subjunctive. When a condition contrary to fact relates to past time, the corresponding compound tenses are used.

> **Si viniesen a vernos, iríamos todos al concierto.**
> If they should come to see us, we should all go to the concert.

> **Si mi primo estuviera (estuviese) aquí, compraría (comprara) la casa.**
> If my cousin were here, he would buy the house.

> **Si hubiéramos (hubiésemos) tenido el dinero, hubiéramos (habríamos) viajado.**
> If we had had the money, we should have traveled.

(*a*) The indicative is used in simple conditions (not *less vivid* nor *contrary to fact*).[2]

Si está aquí, estudia. (*Simple present condition*)	If he is here, he is studying.
Si estaba aquí, estudiaba. (*Simple past condition*)	If he was here, he was studying.
Si está aquí mañana, estudiará. (*Simple future condition*)	If he is here to-morrow, he will study.

152. With hortatory or optative use the subjunctive is quite frequent in occurrence.

Que suba a mi cuarto.	Let him come up to my room.
¡ Viva el general Galdós !	Long live (Hurrah for) General Galdós !
¡ Válgame Dios !	Heaven help me !

---

[1] A less vivid future condition is one which implies that if certain conditions should exist in future time, certain results would follow. **Si yo tuviese bastante tiempo, me pasearía,** *If I should have enough time, I should take a walk.*

[2] **Si,** meaning *if* (not *whether*), cannot be followed by the Fut. Ind., Cond. Ind. or Pres. Subj.

¡ Ojalá que viniesen pronto !   Would that they might come
                                  soon !
¡ Ojalá que no lo hubiera dicho ! Would that I had not said it !

153. In softened assertions. — The -ra imperfect subjunctive is used both in principal and in dependent clauses to express a softened assertion.[1]

Quisiera ir a la ópera.   I should like to go to the
                                 opera.
¿ Pudiera Vd. decirme donde   Could you tell me where the
está la estación?   station is ?
Vd. no debiera hacerlo de ese   You ought not to do it in
modo.   that way.

VERBS

154.   Caber, *to be contained, fit*

PRES. PART. cabiendo; PAST PART. cabido.
PRES. IND. quepo, cabes, cabe, cabemos, cabéis, caben.
PRES. SUBJ. quepa, quepas, quepa, quepamos, quepáis, quepan.
IMPF. IND. cabía, etc.; FUT. IND. cabré, etc.; COND. cabría, etc.
PRET. IND. cupe, cupiste, cupo, cupimos, cupisteis, cupieron.
IMPF. SUBJS. cupiese, etc.; cupiera, etc.; FUT. SUBJ. cupiere,
etc.
IMPERATIVES cabe, cabed.

155.   Dormir, *to sleep*

PRES. PART. durmiendo; PAST PART. dormido.
PRES. IND. duermo, duermes, duerme, dormimos, dormís,
duermen.
PRES. SUBJ. duerma, duermas, duerma, durmamos, durmáis,
duerman.
IMPF. IND. dormía, etc.; FUT. IND. dormiré, etc.; COND.
dormiría, etc.
PRET. IND. dormí, dormiste, durmió, dormimos, dormisteis,
durmieron.

---

[1] The conditional indicative of certain verbs is also used in softened assertions. **Preferiría no ir hoy,** *I should prefer not to go to-day.*

Impf. Subjs. **durmiese,** etc.; **durmiera,** etc.; Fut. Subj. **durmiere,** etc.

Imperatives **duerme,** dormid.

156.   Enviar, *to send*

Pres. Part. enviando; Past Part. enviado.

Pres. Ind. **envío, envías, envía,** enviamos, enviáis, **envían.**

Pres. Subj. **envíe, envíes, envíe,** enviemos, enviéis, **envíen.**

Impf. Ind. enviaba, etc.; Fut. Ind. enviaré, etc.; Cond. enviaría, etc.

Pret. Ind. envié, enviaste, envió, enviamos, enviasteis, enviaron.

Impf. Subjs. enviase, etc.; enviara, etc.; Fut. Subj. enviare, etc.

Imperatives **envía,** enviad.

IDIOMS

157. *Deshacerse de*   To get rid of

Se deshizo de sus malos com-   He got rid of his bad compañeros.   panions.

158. *Darse cuenta de* ⎫   To realize, take into ac-
      Hacerse cargo de ⎭   count

Se dió cuenta (Se hizo cargo)de los   He realized the results of his
resultados de sus hechos.   actions.

159. *De propósito*   Purposely, on purpose

Me dió un golpe de propósito.   He gave me a blow purposely.

A

Valencia, 4 de septiembre de 19—.

Querido Alberto:

Cuando vuelva a los Estados Unidos, tendré mucho que contarle acerca de esta parte de España. Por mucho que escriba ahora, no podré darle una buena idea de esta región.

PUERTA DE LA CATEDRAL DE VALENCIA

CAMPESINOS BAILANDO EN LA HUERTA DE VALENCIA

No creo que haya otro autor que describa este distrito con más exactitud que Blasco Ibáñez en sus novelas. Es muy posible que Vd. las haya leído. ¿ Hay mejor descripción que la suya del Tribunal de las Aguas? Yo me había dicho a mí mismo antes de llegar que, si tuviese la opor- 5 tunidad mientras estuviera en Valencia, asistiría a una sesión de ese tribunal.

De propósito llegué el miércoles para visitar el Tribunal al día siguiente. Este tribunal de los valencianos se reune todos los jueves como en la época de los moros. Iban los 10 moros al mercado los jueves, y por consiguiente éste era el día conveniente para que los jueces considerasen y deci- diesen los pleitos. Si los moros pudieran volver a Valencia ahora, verían escenas bastante semejantes a las de su época. A fin de que los campesinos tengan confianza en 15 las sentencias de los jueces de ese tribunal, se les escoge de entre los campesinos mismos. Cualquiera cosa que digan los jueces, la tienen que cumplir los labradores, por miedo de que se les quite el agua que necesiten para regar sus terrenos. Para ellos el agua es la vida, y si no la reciben, 20 pierden la cosecha.

He asistido a este espectáculo, y le aseguro que vale la pena. Los vestidos de los campesinos, sus ademanes animados, sus voces agitadas, la solemnidad de los jueces vestidos de negro, todo eso me ofreció una escena que 25 nunca olvidaré. Ojalá que Vd. hubiera estado aquí, porque le hubiera gustado mucho.

A donde quiera que se vaya aquí, hay algo que hace pensar en el Cid, quien quitó a los moros esta ciudad. No hay nadie que pueda ver todo eso sin que le entre en el 30 alma un poco del entusiasmo de los españoles por su gran héroe.

No me envíe Vd. más cartas. Estaré de vuelta dentro de poco tiempo.

Su afmo.

Luis

B

I. *Cuestionario*

1. ¿ Era posible que Luis describiese bien a Valencia?
2. ¿ Quién lo ha hecho?   3. ¿ Qué quería ver Luis, mientras estuviera en Valencia?   4. ¿ Por qué llegó a Valencia el miércoles?   5. ¿ Por qué se reunía el tribunal los jueves en la época de los moros?   6. ¿ Qué verían los moros ahora, si pudieran volver?   7. ¿ Qué hacen los campesinos a fin de tener confianza en sus jueces?   8. ¿ De qué tienen miedo los campesinos, si no cumplen las sentencias?
9. ¿ Qué cosas no olvidaría Luis?   10. ¿ En quién se piensa en Valencia?

II. *Temas*

1. Las mejores descripciones de la región de Valencia.
2. Lo que quería ver Luis en Valencia.
3. La llegada de Luis a Valencia.
4. Por qué se reune el tribunal los jueves.
5. La confianza de los campesinos en sus jueces.
6. El miedo de los campesinos.
7. La escena de la sesión del tribunal.
8. El Cid en Valencia.

C

(Use the subjunctive, when possible, instead of the infinitive)

MARY. — Louis, Mrs. Mendoza tells us not to fail to visit the National Library. It is near the Paseo de Recoletos. We must visit it as soon as we are in that part of the city so that Mrs. Mendoza will be pleased.

5   LOUIS. — Captain Martin and I took a walk in the Paseo de Recoletos yesterday, in order that I might see the elegant society of Madrid. For several days I had been looking for some one who might tell me the names

of all the passersby. There is no one, of course, who knows everybody, but Captain Martin knows many people. I happened upon him yesterday. " What would you like to do this afternoon ? " he asked me. I told him that I would go wherever he wished to go. " I should like to go to the 5 Paseo de Recoletos," said he, " unless you are tired." We had a fine time, and I am sleepy to-day. Let John go to the Library with Mrs. Mendoza and you.

MARY. — Are you not ashamed ? Do you realize what you are saying ? I said to Mrs. Mendoza that if we had 10 the opportunity, we would go to the Library. If she should ask me again, I should tell her that you would be delighted to go. . . I do not know what is the matter with you, to-day. Why is it necessary for you to use so many sub- junctives ? Are you doing so purposely ? There is nothing 15 that I detest more than the subjunctive. Would that you might get rid of that habit, and use only the infinitive. Try to do so at least to-morrow.

D

Drill

1. I am looking for a student who writes Spanish well. 2. Charles knows a student who knows how to write it well. 3. Is there any person who can write a foreign language as easily as his own ? 4. I do not believe that it is possible, unless he studies a great deal. 5. If I had the money, I should travel in Spain. 6. If Albert's cousin were here, he would help us. 7. I shall write to him, so that he will know that we are here. 8. Would that he might come ! 9. If he should arrive on Wednesday, we would go to see him. 10. Provided that he gets rid of his house, he will come here at once. 11. Unless we send him a letter purposely, he will not realize what we want. 12. When he returns to this city, he will want to go to the

theater.   13. Let him go to the movies, then he will not
go to sleep.   14. If he had been here last week, we should
have gone several times.   15. You ought to go with him
to the museum.   16. How many chairs were contained
5 (*pret.*) in this room?   17. I do not believe that more
than twenty chairs are contained in it.   18. Do you wish
me to write the names of these persons before he comes?
19. Yes, write them so that we may read them easily.
20. I shall do it without their knowing it.

EXERCISE XV

Infinitives — Present Participles — Past Participles

160. **Infinitives** have only three endings: **-ar,** first conjugation; **-er,** second conjugation; **-ir,** third conjugation.

Hablar, to speak; **comer,** to eat; **escribir,** to write.

161. Use of the infinitive. — The infinitive is used in
Spanish after all prepositions, where in English the present
participle is used.

En vez de venir ayer, me es-
    cribió.
	Instead of coming yesterday,
	    he wrote to me.

Salió sin hablarme.	He left without speaking to me.

162. The infinitive (as a verbal noun) may be used as
the subject or object of a verb.[1]

El viajar es muy agradable.	Traveling is very agreeable.
Mi tía aborrece el fumar.	My aunt abhors smoking.

163. The infinitive is used after impersonal expressions
without any preposition.

---

[1] For the use of the article **el** with the infinitive, see § **3,** 2. **Al (a + el)**
followed by the infinitive, is equivalent to English *on* or *upon* followed
by the present participle, or to a clause. **Al llegar le dió a él su tarjeta de
visita,** *Upon arriving (when he arrived), he gave him his calling card.*

Es preciso trabajar mucho.	It is necessary to work much.
No es difícil olvidar los verbos irregulares.	It is not difficult to forget the irregular verbs.

164. The following are some of the most common verbs which govern the infinitive without any preposition:[1]

creer, *believe*	permitir, *permit*	saber, *know (how)*
esperar, *hope*	poder, *be able*	sentir, *feel, regret*
impedir, *prevent*	procurar, *try*	servirse, *please*
mandar, *order*	prohibir, *prohibit*	temer, *fear*
necesitar *need*	querer, *wish*	

Podrán comprendernos bien.	They will be able to understand us well.
Vds. quieren ir con ellos.	You wish to go with them.
No sabemos hacer ese trabajo.	We do not know how to do that work.

165. Common verbs which require **de** before the infinitive:[1]

acordarse, *remember*	arrepentirse, *repent*	jactarse, *boast*
alegrarse, *be glad*	cesar, *cease*	olvidarse, *forget*
aprovecharse, *profit by*	gozar, *enjoy*	

Se alegró de venir ayer.	He was glad to come yesterday.
Gozamos de tocar la guitarra.	We enjoy playing the guitar.

166. Common verbs which require **a** before the infinitive:[1]

aprender, *learn*	decidirse, *decide*	venir, *come*
apresurarse, *hurry*	enseñar, *teach*	principiar
atreverse, *dare*	ir, *go*	comenzar } *begin*
ayudar, *help*	llegar, *succeed*	empezar

Aprenden a leer.	They are learning to read.
Vamos a visitar a España.	We are going to visit Spain.

167. Common verbs which require **en** before the infinitive:[1]

acordar, *agree*	empeñarse } *insist*	interesarse, *interest oneself*
consistir, *consist*	insistir	
equivocarse, *be mistaken*	fijarse, *pay attention*	tardar, *delay*

---

[1] See Appendix D for list of verbs followed by the infinitive without a preposition, by **a, de, en, por,** and **con.**

Acordaron en hacerlo.	They agreed to do it.
Nos interesamos en oírlos hablar de España.	We are interested in hearing them talk of Spain.

168. The present participle (gerund) is invariable in ending (-ndo). It is expressed in English by a present participle, or by a present participle preceded by a preposition such as *by*, *while*, and *on*.

Diciendo eso, se marchó.	Saying that, he went away.
Se aprende estudiando mucho.	One learns by studying much.
Paseándose en el parque, se encontró con el profesor.	While walking in the park, he met the professor.

169. Use of the present participle. — The present participle is used after the verb **estar**[1] to form a progressive construction in order to emphasize the continuance of an action.[2]

Está hablando todo el tiempo.	He is (keeps) talking all the time.
Estábamos estudiando toda la tarde.	We were studying all the afternoon.

(*a*) Verbs of motion, such as **ir, venir, andar, etc.,** and verbs of rest, such as **quedar,** may be substituted for **estar** in this construction.

Van (están) escribiendo con mucho cuidado.	They are writing very carefully.
Quedan leyendo las revistas.	They keep reading the magazines.

170. Past participle. — The past participles of verbs with infinitives in -ar end in -ado, of verbs with infinitives in -er or -ir, in -ido. When they are used to form the compound tenses with **haber,** they do not vary in ending. Past participles used as adjectives vary for gender and number.

---

[1] See § **14,** 3.

[2] The present participles of **ser, estar, ir,** and **venir** are never used in the progressive construction. **Voy** (not **estoy yendo**) **cada día a mis clases,** *I go (am going) every day to my classes.*

Hemos aprendido a escribir el español.
We have learned to write Spanish.

Aquí están las cartas que Vd. ha escrito.
Here are the letters that you have written.

En esta sala de clase hay dos ventanas abiertas y una cerrada.
In this class room there are two open windows and one closed one.

171. The past participle may be used without any other verb in an absolute construction.

Hecho esto, se decidió a vender
la casa.
This being done, he decided
to sell the house.

Acabado el trabajo del día,
volví a casa.
The day's work being ended,
I returned home.

VERBS

172. Huír, *to flee*

PRES. PART. huyendo; PAST PART. huído.
PRES. IND. huyo, huyes, huye, huímos, huís, huyen.
PRES. SUBJ. huya, huyas, huya, huyamos, huyáis, huyan.
IMPF. IND. huía, etc.; FUT. IND. huiré, etc.; COND. huiría, etc.
PRET. IND. huí, huíste, huyó, huímos, huísteis, huyeron.
IMPF. SUBJS. huyese, etc ; huyera, etc.; FUT. SUBJ. huyere, etc.
IMPERATIVES huye, huíd.

173. Asir, *to seize*

PRES. PART. asiendo; PAST PART. asido.
PRES. IND. asgo, ases, ase, asimos, asís, asen.
PRES. SUBJ. asga, asgas, asga, asgamos, asgáis, asgan.
IMPF. IND. asía, etc.; FUT. IND. asiré, etc.; COND. asiría, etc.
PRET. IND. así, asiste, asió, asimos, asisteis, asieron.
IMPF. SUBJS. asiese, etc.; asiera, etc.; FUT. SUBJ. asiere, etc.
IMPERATIVES ase, asid.

174. Oler, *to smell*

PRES. PART. oliendo; PAST PART. olido.
PRES. IND. huelo, hueles, huele, olemos, oléis, huelen.
PRES. SUBJ. huela, huelas, huela, olamos, oláis, huelan.

Impf. Ind. olía, etc.; Fut. Ind. oleré, etc.; Cond. olería, etc.
Pret. Ind. olí, oliste, olió, olimos, olisteis, olieron.
Impf. Subjs. oliese, etc.; oliera, etc.; Fut. Subj. oliere, etc.
Imperatives huele, oled.

IDIOMS

175. *Hacer efectivo*	To cash (*a check or draft*)
Voy a hacer efectiva mi letra.	I am going to cash my draft.
176. *Al contado*	For cash
Vendemos vestidos sólo al contado.	We sell clothing for cash only.
177. *Al por mayor* (*menor*)	At wholesale (retail)
Compré los géneros al por mayor (al por menor).	I bought the goods at wholesale (at retail).

A

Barcelona, 9 de septiembre de 19—.

Querido Alberto:

Ésta es la última carta que podré escribirle antes de
partir de Barcelona para los Estados Unidos. Vd. sabe,
sin duda, que esta ciudad es el puerto comercial más impor-
5 tante de este país. He visto muchas fábricas aquí. De
este puerto se exporta una gran cantidad de telas de seda y
de algodón, encajes, abanicos, jabones, papel, etc. Hay
aquí muchos comerciantes al por mayor, que envían agentes
comerciales por toda España y al extranjero. También hay
10 tiendas al por menor, en donde se venden artículos de todas
clases. Aquí es fácil hacer efectiva una letra de cambio de
cualquier país, porque los banqueros conocen el valor del
dinero de todos los países.

Esta mañana andaba buscando tiendas en donde se
15 hallasen cosas que pudiese llevar conmigo como recuerdos
de España. Al fin di con una tienda en la cual compré una
bandera nacional, una hermosa faja con los colores nacionales,

pañuelos de seda, corbatas, y encajes bonitísimos. En otra calle tuve la buena suerte de dar con una tienda en cuyo escaparate se hallaban muchas figurillas de barro que representaban toreros y toros. Había un grupo de la cuadrilla entera, otro de banderilleros, capeadores y picadores con un 5 toro, y otro de un matador con un toro. Un picador asiendo fuertemente su garrocha estaba para picar un toro; un capeador huía del toro que le perseguía, y el toro olía la capa caída de la mano del capeador; un matador tenía levantada la mano con el estoque para recibir el ataque del 10 toro. Me decidí a comprar estas figurillas, porque no hay mejor modo de representar a lo vivo a mis amigos en América una corrida de toros en España. Me las vendieron baratas porque ofrecí pagar al contado. Para que no se quebrasen, las empaquetaron en cajitas con mucho cuidado.   15

Ya pienso en volver a los Estados Unidos, y no tardaré mucho en ir a visitarle. Cuando le vea, espero probarle que sé hablar español mucho mejor a causa de mi viaje por España.

Siempre su afmo.

Luis

B

I. *Cuestionario*

1. ¿Cuántas otras cartas escribirá Luis desde España? 2. ¿Por qué es importante Barcelona? 3. ¿Qué exporta? 4. ¿Que clases de tiendas hay? 5. ¿Por qué no es difícil hacer efectiva una letra de cambio? 6. ¿Qué andaba buscando Luis? 7. ¿Qué compró en la primera tienda? 8. ¿Con qué dió en la segunda tienda? 9. ¿Por qué compró las figurillas? 10. ¿Por qué habla mejor Luis ahora?

II. *Temas*

1. La última carta.   3. Las tiendas al por mayor
2. El comercio de Barcelona.   y al por menor.

4. Los banqueros y las letras de cambio.

5. La primera tienda y las compras de Luis.

6. La segunda tienda y sus figurillas.

7. Lo que parecían hacer las figurillas.

8. Las razones para comprarlas.

9. El cuidado en empaquetarlas.

10. La vuelta de Luis a los Estados Unidos.

C

(Use the infinitive, whenever possible, instead of the subjunctive)

MARY. — Why do you insist on singing all the time, Louis? I cannot do anything. Please stop singing at once; I can stand no more. Singing always bores me. Are you so glad to leave Spain for America? I am very sorry to go
5 away. It is a pity that John is not going with us. Do you think that he will delay in coming to see us to-day?

LOUIS. — Doubtless John is busy now buying souvenirs of Spain for you. While walking along the street, I saw him in a shop. He was buying enough to obtain wholesale
10 prices. Things are cheap in this city, even when one buys at retail, provided that he pays cash. Are you not afraid that John will be unable to study history without you? He cannot study it well without your being here to help him.

15 MARY. — My goodness! You are using subjunctives again! . . . Oh, there comes John. Louis, my mother wants you to help pack the trunks, at once. She does not allow me to help, although I should like to do so. Will you tell me later, Louis, what she has in the trunks for
20 me; — fans, lace, a silk dress, or whatever it may be?

JOHN. — I am sorry that you have to go now, Louis. Think of me when you are seasick on the Atlantic. Do not forget to eat much. Remember your uncle, the famous doctor, who ordered you to eat a great deal on the boat.

Louis. — I know well that you (*pl.*) are trying to get rid of me. It doesn't matter. I have to cash a draft at [1] the bank. I shall certainly see you to-morrow, John. I do not believe that you will forget to come to the boat. It would be a pity for you to fail to say " Goodbye " to — 5 Mary's mother.

D

Drill

1. Albert, how does one say in Spanish, " The general fled; let us flee." ?   2. What do you intend to do to-day, after the Spanish class?   3. I intend to go to the bank to cash a check for fifty dollars.   4. My father forgot to send it to me last week.   5. He did not remember to do it although I wrote to him every day.   6. Well, I hope that you will not delay in paying me what you owe me. 7. You have owed me ten dollars for a month, for the silk ties which I bought for you.   8. I was able to obtain them at wholesale by paying cash.   9. The colors will not fail to please you; — red (*sing.*), yellow, and green. 10. I am fond of bright colors, but I shall not dare to wear the ties to-morrow.   11. My father and mother are coming to see me.   12. My mother has just sent me some flowers.   13. They smell good; I want you to smell them.   14. Do not grasp them so tightly.   15. My father wrote me that my mother was busy packing the trunk.   16. I am going to ask my father to allow me to go to Spain or South America next summer.   17. One learns a great deal by traveling.   18. Are you able now to write to your friends in Spanish?

---

[1] en.

APPENDIX A

Accentuation and Syllabication

1. Accentuation.

1. Words ending in a consonant,[1] except **n** or **s**, are stressed on the last syllable.

Español, *Spanish;* **comprar,** *to buy;* **ciudad,** *city;* **reloj,** *watch;* **nariz,** *nose.*

2. Words ending in a vowel (including diphthongs [2]) or in **n** or **s** are stressed on the next to the last syllable.[3]

Casa, *house;* **hombre,** *man;* **libro,** *book;* **compran,** *they buy;* **pedimos,** *we ask;* **familia,** *family;* **sabio,** *wise.*

3. Any exception to rule 1 or 2 above (including stress on a syllable preceding the next to the last one) requires a written accent on the stressed syllable.[4]

Fácil, *easy;* **lápiz,** *pencil;* **sofá,** *sofa;* **café,** *coffee;* **habló,** *he spoke;* **nación,**[5] *nation;* **inglés,**[5] *English;* **día,** *day;* **tenía,** *he had;* **exámenes,**[6] *examinations;* **telégrafo,** *telegraph.*

4. The written accent must be used to distinguish visually words similar in spelling and pronunciation but different in meaning or function.

---

[1] Final **y** is considered as a consonant for accentual purposes, although it sounds as a vowel. **Paraguay, Uruguay.**

[2] A few diphthongal monosyllables bear the written accent: **fuí, fué, dió, vió.** However, there is no accent on **vais, dais** and **deis.**

[3] However, a verb retains its written accent when a pronoun is affixed to it. **Dé Vd.,** *give;* **dénos Vd.,** *give us.*

[4] A verb not accented when standing alone adds a written accent when a pronoun is affixed, in case the stress then falls on a syllable preceding the next to the last. **Diciendo,** *saying,* **diciéndonoslo,** *saying it to us.*

[5] The addition of **-es** to form the plural results in the loss of the written accent, when it is on the final syllable. **Nación, naciones; inglés, ingleses; jardín, jardines.**

[6] The addition of **-es** to form the plural of nouns stressed on the next to the last syllable makes a written accent necessary. **Examen, exámenes; orden, órdenes.**

aquel, that (*adjective*)	aquél, that one (*pronoun*)
como, as	¿ cómo ? how ? ¡ cómo ! how !
cual, as, which, etc.	¿ cuál ? which ?
cuando, when	¿ cuándo ? when ?
cuanto, as much (many) as	¿ cuánto ? how much (many) ?
de, of, from	dé, give (*Pres. Subj.*)
donde, where	¿ dónde ? where ?
el, the	él, he
ese, that (*adjective*)	ése, that one (*pronoun*)
este, this (*adjective*)	éste, this one (*pronoun*)
mas, but	más, more
mi, my	mí, me
que, that, etc.	¿ qué ? what ?
quien, who	¿ quién ? who ?
se, himself, etc.	sé, I know, be (*imperative*)
si, if	sí, yes, himself, etc.
solo, alone	sólo, only
tu, your (*familiar*)	tú, you (*familiar*)

2. Diphthongs and triphthongs.

1. *Diphthongs.* — A diphthong is a combination of two vowels to form a single syllable. Contrary to English, the sound of each vowel of a diphthong in Spanish is distinctly heard. A diphthong consists of a combination of (1) a strong vowel [1] (a, e, o) and a weak vowel (i, y, u) or (2) of two weak vowels.[2] In (1) the stress falls on the strong vowel; in (2) the stress falls on the second weak vowel. The following combinations are found: —

Strong and Weak Vowel		Weak and Strong Vowel		Two Weak Vowels	
ai (y)	aire, hay	ia	viaje	iu	ciudad
au	causa	ie	quien	ui	fuimos
oi (y)	oigo, hoy	io	estudio		
ou	Sousa	ua	cuando		
ei (y)	reina, rey	ue	puesto		
eu	Europa	uo	cuota		

[1] Two contiguous strong vowels never unite into a single syllable. **Ca-er, le-er, po-e-ma.**

[2] In case the first of two contiguous weak vowels is stressed or a weak vowel standing next to a strong one, two separate syllables are formed, and this stress is indicated by a written accent. **Cre-í-a, dí-a, flú-i-do.**

2. *Triphthongs.* — A triphthong consists of a strong vowel between two weak vowels. The stress falls on the strong vowel. The following combinations are found:

iai	estudiáis
iei	enviéis
uai (y)	averiguáis, Uruguay
uei (y)	averigüéis, buey

3. Syllabication.

1. A single consonant (including **ch, ll, rr**) between vowels goes with the following vowel. **Lá-piz, ve-ra-no, mu-cha-cho, ca-ba-llo, pe-rro.**

2. Two adjacent consonants are regularly divided, so that one goes with each syllable. **Per-so-na, lec-ción, tin-ta, her-mo-so.** However, consonants followed by l or r (except **rl, sl, tl, sr**) are not separated. **Ma-dre, a-ma-ble, cua-tro, si-glo, li-bro, (At-lán-ti-co, mer-lu-za).**

3. When more than two consonants occur between vowels, only the last consonant or the two consonants of the inseparable groups mentioned in rule 2 above go with the following syllable. **Ex-pli-car, sor-pre-sa, trans-po-ner, mez-cla.**

4. Prefixes are usually inseparable, even if in violation of the above rules. **Des-es-pe-rar, sub-le-var, des-a-tar.**

APPENDIX B

Verb Formation

I. THE REGULAR CONJUGATIONS

I	II	III

Infinitive Mode

compr **ar,** *to buy*	vend **er,** *to sell*	viv **ir,** *to live*

Participles

PRESENT

compr **ando,** *buying*	vend **iendo,** *selling*	viv **iendo,** *living*

PAST

compr **ado,** *bought*	vend **ido,** *sold*	viv **ido,** *lived*

Indicative Mode

PRESENT

I buy, do buy, am buying, etc.	*I sell, do sell, am selling, etc.*	*I live, do live, am living, etc.*
compr **o**	vend **o**	viv **o**
compr **as**	vend **es**	viv **es**
compr **a**	vend **e**	viv **e**
compr **amos**	vend **emos**	viv **imos**
compr **áis**	vend **éis**	viv **ís**
compr **an**	vend **en**	viv **en**

IMPERFECT (PAST DESCRIPTIVE)

I was buying, used to buy, bought, etc.	*I was selling, used to sell, sold, etc.*	*I was living, used to live, lived, etc.*
compr **aba**	vend **ía**	viv **ía**
compr **abas**	vend **ías**	viv **ías**
compr **aba**	vend **ía**	viv **ía**

compr ábamos	vend íamos	viv íamos
compr abais	vend íais	viv íais
compr aban	vend ían	viv ían

PRETERITE (PAST ABSOLUTE)

I bought, etc.	*I sold, etc.*	*I lived, etc.*
compr é	vend í	viv í
compr aste	vend iste	viv iste
compr ó	vend ió	viv ió
compr amos	vend imos	viv imos
compr asteis	vend isteis	viv isteis
compr aron	vend ieron	viv ieron

FUTURE

I shall buy, etc.	*I shall sell, etc.*	*I shall live, etc.*
comprar é	vender é	vivir é
comprar ás	vender ás	vivir ás
comprar á	vender á	vivir á
comprar emos	vender emos	vivir emos
comprar éis	vender éis	vivir éis
comprar án	vender án	vivir án

CONDITIONAL (PAST FUTURE)

I should buy, etc.	*I should sell, etc.*	*I should live, etc.*
comprar ía	vender ía	vivir ía
comprar ías	vender ías	vivir ías
comprar ía	vender ía	vivir ía
comprar íamos	vender íamos	vivir íamos
comprar íais	vender íais	vivir íais
comprar ían	vender ían	vivir ían

Imperative Mode

Buy	*Sell*	*Live*
compr a (tú)	vend e (tú)	viv e (tú)
compr ad (vosotros, -as)	vend ed (vosotros, -as)	viv id (vosotros, -as)

Subjunctive Mode

PRESENT

(*That I may*) buy, (*let me*) buy, etc.	(*That I may*) sell, (*let me*) sell, etc.	(*That I may*) live, (*let me*) live, etc.
compr e	vend a	viv a
compr es	vend as	viv as
compr e	vend a	viv a
compr emos	vend amos	viv amos
compr éis	vend áis	viv áis
compr en	vend an	viv an

IMPERFECT (PAST)

(-se form)

(*That*) I might or should buy, etc.	(*That*) I might or should sell, etc.	(*That*) I might or should live, etc.
compr ase	vend iese	viv iese
compr ases	vend ieses	viv ieses
compr ase	vend iese	viv iese
compr ásemos	vend iésemos	viv iésemos
compr aseis	vend ieseis	viv ieseis
compr asen	vend iesen	viv iesen

IMPERFECT (PAST)

(-ra form)

(*That*) I might or should buy, etc.	(*That*) I might or should sell, etc.	(*That*) I might or should live, etc.
compr ara	vend iera	viv iera
compr aras	vend ieras	viv ieras
compr ara	vend iera	viv iera
compr áramos	vend iéramos	viv iéramos
compr arais	vend ierais	viv ierais
compr aran	vend ieran	viv ieran

Future

(or Hypothetical)

That I (may or shall) buy, etc.	*That I (may or shall) sell, etc.*	*That I (may or shall) live, etc.*
compr **are**	vend **iere**	viv **iere**
compr **ares**	vend **ieres**	viv **ieres**
compr **are**	vend **iere**	viv **iere**
compr **áremos**	vend **iéremos**	viv **iéremos**
compr **areis**	vend **iereis**	viv **iereis**
compr **aren**	vend **ieren**	viv **ieren**

II. THE COMPOUND TENSES

The compound tenses of all verbs, regular and irregular, are formed by adding their past participle (invariable) to the proper form of the auxiliary **haber,** *to have* (see § 6).[1]

Model verb with **haber**

Infinitive	Participle
PRESENT PERFECT	PRESENT PERFECT
haber comprado, *to have bought*	**habiendo comprado,** *having bought*

Indicative

PRESENT PERFECT
he comprado, etc., *I have bought, etc.*

PLUPERFECT (PAST PERFECT)
había comprado, etc., *I had bought, etc.*

PAST ANTERIOR (SECOND PAST PERFECT)
hube comprado, etc., *I had bought, etc.*

---

[1] The passive voice is formed with **ser,** *to be* (see § 15), and the past participle (variable) of the verb.

FUTURE PERFECT

habré comprado, etc., *I shall have bought, etc.*

CONDITIONAL PERFECT

habría comprado, etc., *I should have bought, etc.*

Subjunctive

PRESENT PERFECT

haya comprado, etc., *(that) I may have bought, etc.*

PLUPERFECT (PAST PERFECT)

(**-se** form)

hubiese comprado, etc., *(that) I might have bought, etc.*

PLUPERFECT (PAST PERFECT)

(**-ra** form)

hubiera comprado, etc., *(that) I might have bought, etc.*

FUTURE PERFECT

hubiere comprado, etc., *that I (may* or *shall) have bought, etc.*

III. ORTHOGRAPHIC–CHANGING VERBS

1. Changes which occur before **e** of the ending (to preserve the consonantal sound at the end of the stem of the infinitive).[1]

1. In -car verbs **c>qu**:

    Sacar — *Pret. Ind. 1st sing.* **saqué**
               Pres. Subj. **saque, saques, saque, saquemos, saquéis, saquen**

2. In -gar verbs **g>gu**:

    Pagar — *Pret. Ind. 1st sing.* **pagué**
               Pres. Subj. **pague, pagues, pague, paguemos, paguéis, paguen**

---

[1] Only seven forms of the verb inflection are affected by the consonantal changes mentioned in group 1.

3. In -guar verbs gu>gü:

    Averiguar — *Pret. Ind. 1st sing.* averigüé
               Pres. Subj. averigüe, averigües, averigüe, averi-
                       güemos, averigüéis, averigüen

4. In -zar verbs z>c:

    Gozar — *Pret. Ind. 1st sing.* gocé
           Pres. Subj. goce, goces, goce, gocemos, gocéis, gocen

2. Changes which occur before o or a of the ending (to pre-serve the consonantal sound at the end of the stem of the infinitive).[1]

1. In -cer and -cir verbs preceded by a consonant c>z:

    Vencer — *Pres. Ind. 1st sing.* venzo
             Pres. Subj. venza, venzas, venza, venzamos, ven-
                 záis, venzan

    Esparcir — *Pres. Ind. 1st sing.* esparzo
              Pres. Subj. esparza, esparzas, esparza, esparzamos,
                   esparzáis, esparzan

   (a) In -cer and -cir verbs preceded by a vowel c>zc (differs from
      stem):

    Conocer — *Pres. Ind. 1st sing.* conozco
             Pres. Subj. conozca, conozcas, conozca, conozca-
                 mos, conozcáis, conozcan

    Lucir — *Pres. Ind. 1st sing.* luzco
             Pres. Subj. luzca, luzcas, luzca, luzcamos, luzcáis,
                 luzcan

2. In -ger and -gir verbs g>j:

    Coger — *Pres. Ind. 1st sing.* cojo
             Pres. Subj. coja, cojas, coja, cojamos, cojáis, cojan

    Dirigir — *Pres. Ind. 1st sing.* dirijo
              Pres. Subj. dirija, dirijas, dirija, dirijamos, dirijáis,
                 dirijan

3. In -guir verbs gu>g:

    Distinguir — *Pres. Ind. 1st sing.* distingo
               Pres. Subj. distinga, distingas, distinga, distin-
                    gamos, distingáis, distingan

---

[1] Only seven forms of the verb inflection are affected by the consonantal changes mentioned in group 1.

4. In -quir verbs qu>c:

> **Delinquir** — *Pres. Ind. 1st sing.* delinco
> *Pres. Subj.* delinca, delincas, delinca, delincamos, delincáis, delincan

3. Changes in **-iar** and **-uar** verbs. Certain verbs in **-iar** and **-uar** take a written accent on the **i** or **u** of the stem in the following forms:

> **Envíar** — *Pres. Ind.* envío, envías, envía, envían
> *Pres. Subj.* envíe, envíes, envíe, envíen
> *Imperative singular* envía

> **Continuar** — *Pres. Ind.* continúo, continúas, continúa, continúan
> *Pres. Subj.* continúe, continúes, continúe, continúen
> *Imperative singular* continúa

4. Change of **i** to **y** of the endings **-ie-** and **-ió** in verbs whose stem ends in a vowel (excluding **-iar** and **-uar** verbs).

> **Creer** — *Pres. Part.* creyendo
> *Pret. Ind. 3rd sing. and 3rd pl.* creyó, creyeron
> *Impf. Subjs.* creyese, etc.; creyera, etc.
> *Fut. Subj.* creyere, etc.

5. Loss of **i** of the endings **-ie-** and **-ió** when the stem of the verb ends in **ll**, **ñ** or **j**.

> **Bullir** — *Pres. Part.* bullendo
> *Pret. Ind. 3rd sing. 3rd pl.* bulló, bulleron
> *Impf. Subjs.* bullese, etc.; bullera, etc.
> *Fut. Subj.* bullere, etc.

> **Bruñir** — *Pres. Part.* bruñendo
> *Pret. Ind. 3rd sing. and 3rd pl.* bruñó, bruñeron
> *Impf. Subjs.* bruñese, etc.; bruñera, etc.
> *Fut. Subj.* bruñere, etc.

> **Decir** — *Pret. Ind.* dijo, dijeron
> *Impf. Subjs.* dijese, etc.; dijera, etc.
> *Fut. Subj.* dijere, etc.

6. Verbs ending in **-uír** (not **-guir** and **-quir**) insert **y** at the end of the stem in certain forms, and also change **i** to **y** in the ending, as in group 4 above.

Huír — *Pres. Part.* huyendo
   Pres. Ind. huyo, huyes, huye, huyen
   Pres. Subj. huya huyas, huya, huyamos, huyáis huyan
   Imperative singular huye
   Pret. Ind. 3rd sing. and 3rd pl. huyó, huyeron
   Impf. Subjs. huyese, etc.; huyera, etc.
   Fut. Subj. huyere, etc.

IV. RADICAL–CHANGING VERBS

1. Class I (-ar and -er verbs). — If stressed, the stem vowel **e > ie** and **o > ue.** It occurs in only nine forms.

Pensar — *Pres. Ind.* pienso, piensas, piensa, piensan
   Pres. Subj. piense, pienses, piense, piensen
   Imperative singular piensa

Contar[1] — *Pres. Ind.* cuento, cuentas, cuenta, cuentan
   Pres. Subj. cuente, cuentes, cuente, cuenten
   Imperative singular cuenta

Perder — *Pres. Ind.* pierdo, pierdes, pierde, pierden
   Pres. Subj. pierda, pierdas, pierda, pierdan
   Imperative singular pierde

Volver — *Pres. Ind.* vuelvo, vuelves, vuelve, vuelven
   Pres. Subj. vuelva, vuelvas, vuelva, vuelvan
   Imperative singular vuelve

(*a*) If initial vowels are stressed, **e > ye,** and **o > hue.**

Errar — *Pres. Ind.* yerro, yerras, yerra, yerran
   Pres. Subj. yerre, yerres, yerre, yerren
   Imperative singular yerra

Oler — *Pres. Ind.* huelo, hueles, huele, huelen
   Pres. Subj. huela, huelas, huela, huelan
   Imperative singular huele

---

[1] **Jugar** (originally **jogar**) is inflected like **contar.**

2. Class II (-ir verbs). [1] — If stressed, the stem vowel
e >ie and o >ue, and also e >i and o >u if unstressed, in
case the following syllable begins with -a-, -ie- or -ió.

Sentir — *Pres. Part.*   sintiendo
Pres. Ind.   siento, sientes, siente, sienten
Pres. Subj.   sienta, sientas, sienta, sintamos, sintáis, sientan
Imperative singular   siente
Pret. Ind.   sintió, sintieron
Impf. Subjs.   sintiese, etc.; sintiera, etc.
Fut. Subj.   sintiere, etc.

Dormir — *Pres. Part.*   durmiendo
Pres. Ind.   duermo, duermes, duerme, duermen
Pres. Subj.   duerma, duermas, duerma, durmamos, durmáis, duermen
Imperative singular   duerme
Pret. Ind.   durmió, durmieron
Impf. Subjs.   durmiese, etc.; durmiera, etc.
Fut. Subj.   durmiere, etc.

3. Class III (-ir verbs). [2] — If stressed, the stem vowel e >i,
and also e >i if unstressed, in case the following syllable begins
with -a-, -ie- or -ió.

Pedir — *Pres. Part.*   pidiendo
Pres. Ind.   pido, pides, pide, piden
Pres. Subj.   pida, pidas, pida, pidamos, pidáis, pidan
Imperative singular   pide
Pret. Ind.   pidió, pidieron
Impf. Subjs.   pidiese, etc.; pidiera, etc.
Fut. Subj.   pidiere, etc.

---

[1] Class II contains all verbs ending in -entir, -erir, and -ertir, as well
as hervir.

[2] To class III belong all verbs ending in -ebir, -edir, -egir, -eguir, -eír,
-emir, -enchir, -endir, -eñir, -estir and -etir, as well as servir.

APPENDIX C

Reference List of Irregular Verbs

The numbers below in black faced type indicate paragraphs in the text where the complete conjugation of the verb is to be found; the numbers in light faced type indicate the model verb. The vowels in black faced type in the parentheses indicate the radical change which occurs. The capital letter B, after a verb, refers to Appendix B; the Roman and Arabic numerals following B refer to sections of the Appendix. *Suppl.* refers to the Supplement to Exercise I which treats of verb formation.

A

abrir	*Suppl.* C, VIII	
acertar (**ie**)		88
acordar(se) (**ue**)		134
acostar(se) (**ue**)		**134**
advertir (**ie**)		102
almorzar (**ue**)		134
andar		**54**
aprobar (**ue**)		134
argüir	B, III, 6	172
arrepentirse (**ie**)		102
asir		**173**
atraer		89
atravesar (**ie**)		88

B

bruñir	B, III, 5	
bullir	B, III, 5	

C

caber		**154**
caer		**142**
calentar (**ie**)		88

ceñir (**i**)	B, III, 5	114
cerrar (**ie**)		88
cocer (**ue**)		78
colegir (**i**)	B, III, 2	114
colgar (**ue**)		134
comenzar (**ie**)		88
competir (**i**)		116
componer		40
concluír	B, III, 6	172
conducir		**135**
confesar (**ie**)		88
conocer		**126**
conseguir (**i**)	B, III, 2	124
consentir (**ie**)		102
construír	B, III, 6	172
contar (**ue**)		**134**
contener		7
contribuír	B, III, 6	172
convenir		67
convertir (**ie**)		102
corregir (**i**)	B, III, 2	124
costar (**ue**)		134
creer		B, III, 4
cubrir		*Suppl.* C, VIII

D

dar	**77**
decir	**28**
defender (ie)	*Suppl.* A, I
demostrar (ue)	134
descender (ie)	*Suppl.* A, I
despedir (i)	114
despertar (ie)	88
destruír	B, III, 6 172
devolver (ue)	78
disminuír	B, III, 6 172
disponer	40
distribuír	B, III, 6 172
divertir (ie)	102
dormir (ue)	155

E

elegir (i)	114
empezar (ie)	88
encender (ie)	*Suppl.* A, I
encontrar (ue)	134
entender (ie)	*Suppl.* A, I
enviar	B, III, 3 156
envolver (ue)	78
errar	B, IV, 1 (*a*)
escribir	*Suppl.* C, VIII
estar	**16**

G

gemir (i)	114

H

haber	**6**
hacer	**27**
helar (ie)	88
herir (ie)	102
hervir (ie)	102
huír	**172**

I

impedir (i)	114
imponer	40
imprimir	*Suppl.* C, VIII
incluír	B, III, 6 172
inducir	B, III, 5 135
introducir	B, III, 5 135
ir	**53**

J

jugar	**136**

L

leer	B, III, 4
lucir	B, III, 2 126

Ll

llover (ue)	78

M

manifestar (ie)	88
medir (i)	114
mentir (ie)	102
morir	**125**
mostrar (ue)	134
mover (ue)	78

N

negar (ie)	88
nevar (ie)	88

O

obtener	7
oír	**143**
oler (ue)	**174**

P

parecer	126
pedir (i)	**114**

APPENDIX D

List of verbs governing the direct infinitive or requiring the prepositions **a, de, en, por** or **con** before a dependent infinitive.

A

abandonar(se) **a,** to give (oneself) up to

abstenerse **de,** to refrain from

acabar **de,** to finish, to have just; — **por,** to end by

acceder **a,** to accede, agree to

acomodarse **a,** to conform to

aconsejar —, to advise to

acordarse **de,** to remember

acostumbrar —, to be used to; —(se) **a,** to become used to

acudir **a,** to hasten to, go, come

acusar **de,** to accuse of

adherir(se) **a,** to stick to

afanarse **por,** to exert oneself to

aficionarse **a,** to become addicted to

afirmar —, to affirm, declare

afligirse **de,** to lament

agraviarse **de,** to be grieved at

ajustarse **a,** to agree to

alcanzar **a,** to reach, attain to

alegrarse **de,** to be glad to

amenazar —, to threaten to; — **con,** to threaten with

anhelar —, to long to

animar **a,** to encourage to

aplicarse **a,** to apply oneself to

aprender **a,** to learn to

apresurar(se) **a,** to hurry; hasten to

aprovecharse **de,** to profit by

apurarse **por,** to exert oneself to

arrepentirse **de,** to repent of

arriesgar **con,** to risk by

asegurar —, to assure, claim to

aspirar **a,** to aspire to

asustarse **de,** to be frightened at

atreverse **a,** to dare to

autorizar **a,** to authorize to

aventurarse **a,** to venture to

avergonzarse **de,** to be ashamed of

ayudar **a,** to aid, help to

B

bastar **con,** to be enough to

C

cansar(se) **de,** to tire, make (grow) weary of

celebrar —, to be glad to

cesar **de,** to cease to

comenzar **a,** to begin, commence to

complacerse **en,** to take pleasure in

comprometer(se) **a,** to engage (oneself), agree to

condenar **a,** to condemn to

condescender **a,** to condescend to

conducir **a,** to lead, conduct to

confesar —, to confess

confiar **en,** to trust, hope to

conformarse **a,** to conform, agree to

consagrar(se) **a,** to devote (oneself) to

conseguir —, to succeed in

consentir **en,** to consent to

consistir **en,** to consist in

conspirar **a,** to conspire to

consumirse **en,** to be consumed in

contar **con,** to count on

contentarse **con,** to content oneself with; — **de,** to be satisfied to

continuar **a,** to continue to

contribuír **a,** to contribute to

convenir(se) —, en, *or* a, to agree to

convidar a, to invite to

correr a, to run to

creer —, to believe, think

D

dar a, to give to; —se a, to give oneself up to

deber —, ought to, should; — de, ought to, must (*supposition*)

decidir(se) — *or* a, to decide to

declarar —, to declare

dedicar(se) a, to dedicate, devote (oneself) to

dejar —, to let, allow, permit to; — de, to cease to, stop

deleitarse en, to take delight in

desafiar a, to challenge to

descender a, to descend to

descuidar de, to neglect to

desdeñar(se) — *or* de, to disdain to

desear —, to desire, wish to

desesperar(se) de, to despair of

desistir de, to desist from

destinar a, to destine to

detenerse a, to stop to

determinarse a, to determine to

dignarse — *or* de, to deign to

disculpar(se) de, to excuse oneself for

dispensar de, to excuse from

disponer(se) a, to get ready, prepare to

disuadir de, to dissuade from

divertirse en *or* con, to amuse oneself by *or* with

dudar —, to doubt; — en, to hesitate to

E

echar(se) a, to begin to

elegir —, to choose to

empeñarse en, to insist on

empezar a, to begin to

encargarse de, to undertake to

enseñar a, to teach to

entrar a, to enter on, begin to

entretener(se) a, to entertain oneself by *or* with

enviar a, to send to

equivocarse en, to be mistaken in

escuchar —, to listen to

esforzar(se) a, en *or* por, to attempt to

esmerarse en, to take pains in

esperar —, to hope to

estar para, to be about to; — por, to be inclined to

evitar —, to avoid

excitar a, to excite to

excusar(se) de, to excuse (oneself) from

exhortar a, to exhort to

exponer(se) a, to expose (oneself) to

F

fastidiar(se) de, to weary, be weary of

fatigar(se) de, to tire, be tired of

felicitar(se) de, to congratulate (oneself) on

fijarse en, to pay attention to

fingir —, to pretend to

forzar a, to force to

G

gozar(se) de, to enjoy; —(se) en, to take pleasure in

guardarse de, to guard against

H

haber de, to have to

habituar(se) a, to accustom (oneself) to

hacer —, to make, have; — por, to try to

hartarse de, to be sated with

humillar(se) a, to humiliate (oneself) to

I

imaginarse —, to imagine
impedir —, to prevent, hinder
impeler a, to impel to
incitar a, to incite to
inclinar a, to induce to; —se a, to be inclined to
incomodarse de, to be annoyed at; — por, to put oneself out to
indignarse de, to be indignant at
inducir a, to induce to
insistir en, to insist on
inspirar a, to inspire to
intentar —, to try, attempt
invitar a, to invite to
ir a, to go to

J

jactarse de, to boast of
jurar —, to swear to
justificar(se) de, to justify (oneself) for

L

librar de, to free from
limitar(se) a, to limit (oneself) to
lograr —, to succeed in

Ll

llegar a, to come to, succeed in

M

mandar —, to command, have; — a, to send to
matarse por, to try hard to
meditar en, to meditate upon
merecer —, to deserve to
meterse a, to undertake to
mezclarse en, to take part in
mirar —, to look at
morirse por, to be dying to

N

necesitar —, to need to
negar —, to deny; —se a, to decline, refuse to

O

obligar(se) a, to oblige (oneself) to
obstinarse en, to persist in
ocupar(se) en, to busy (oneself) with or in
odiar —, to hate to
ofrecer(se) —, to offer, promise to; —(se) a, to offer to
oír —, to hear
olvidar —, to forget to; —(se) de, to forget to
oponerse a, to be opposed to
ordenar —, to order to

P

pararse a, to stop to
parecer —, to seem to
particularizarse en, to specialize in
pasar a, to proceed, pass to
pensar —, to intend to; — en, to think of
permitir —, to permit to
perseverar en, to persevere in
persistir en, to persist in
persuadir(se) a, to persuade (oneself) to
poder —, to be able to, can, may
poner a, to put to; —se a, to begin to
preciarse de, to boast of
preferir —, to prefer to
preparar(se) a, to prepare
presumir —, to presume to
pretender —, to pretend, try to
principiar a, to begin to
privar(se) de, to deprive, be deprived of
probar a, to try to
proceder a, to proceed to
procurar —, to try to
prohibir —, to forbid
prometer —, to promise to
proponer —, to propose to
provocar a, to provoke to
pugnar por, to strive, struggle for

Q

quedar(se) a, to remain to; — en to agree to; — por, to be considered as

quejarse de, to complain of

querer —, to wish to

R

rabiar por, to be crazy to

recelarse —, to fear

recomendar —, to recommend to

reconocer —, to acknowledge, confess to

recordar —, remember

recrear(se) en, to divert (oneself) by

reducir(se) a, to bring (oneself) to

rehusar(se)— or a to refuse to

renunciar a, to renounce

resignarse a, to resign oneself, submit to

resistirse a, to resist

resolver(se) a, to resolve, decide to

reventar por, to be bursting to

S

saber —, to know how, be able to, can

salir a, to go out to

sentarse a, to sit down to

sentir —, to regret, be sorry to

ser de, to be

servirse —, to please, be so kind as to

sobresalir en, to excel in

soler —, to be used, accustomed to

soltar a, to start to

someter(se) a, to submit (oneself) to

soñar con, to dream of

sospechar de, to suspect of

sostener —, to maintain, affirm

subir a, to go up to

sugerir —, to suggest

T

tardar en, to delay, be long in

temer —, to fear to

terminar en, to end by

tornar a, to return to, to . . . again

tratar de, to try to

V

vacilar en, to hesitate to

valerse de, to avail oneself of

venir a, to come to

ver —, to see

volar a, to fly to

volver a, to return to, to . . . again

*VOCABULARIES

The Spanish-English vocabulary is above, the English-Spanish below the dividing line. The radical-changing verbs are shown by (ie), (ue), and (i) placed after the verb. If a verb is followed by an infinitive without a preposition, it is shown by (—); if a preposition is required, (a), (de), (en), (por), (con) are used. The numbers refer to paragraphs.

a to, at, on; — **caballo** on horseback; — **fin de** (+ *infin.*) in order to, so as to; — **fin de que** (+ *subj.*) so that; — **la vez** at the same time; — **lo lejos** in the distance; — **menudo** often; — **pesar de** in spite of; **al** (+ *infin.*) on, upon (+ *pres. part.*); **al fin** finally; **al** (**a lo, por lo**) **menos** at least; **al por mayor** (at) wholesale; **al por menor** (at) retail

abajo below; **más —,** lower down

abanico *m.* fan

abierto, -a open

abogado *m.* lawyer, advocate

abrir(se) (Suppl. Ex. 1, C, VIII) open

abundante abundant, plentiful

acá here

acabar(se) finish, end; **de** (+ *infin.*) have just (+ *past part.*)

acerca de about, concerning, in regard to

acercarse (a) (App. B, III, 1) approach

acometer attack

acompañar accompany, go with

acordarse (ue) (de) **134** remember

acostarse (ue) **134** go to bed

actor *m.* actor

acudir (a) hasten to, come (go) up to

acuerdo *m.* agreement; **estar (16) de —,** agree

achaque *m.* infirmity

adelantar improve

adelfa *f.* oleander

ademán gesture, manner

adiós goodbye

admiración *f.* admiration

adorno *m.* ornament

aficionado, -a (a) fond (of)

aficionado *m.* enthusiast

afmo. = **afectísimo** very affectionate

agente *m.* agent; — **comercial** salesman

agitar agitate, wave

---

a un *m.,* **una** *f.*

able: be —, poder (—) **66**

aboard: all —! ¡ señores viajeros al tren!

about (*concerning*) acerca de; (*approximately*) poco más o menos, cosa de; **be — to** estar (**16**) para

accident accidente *m.*

accomplish hacer **27,** lograr

accordingly por eso, por lo tanto, por consiguiente

acquaintance: make — of conocer **126**

acquainted: be — with conocer **126**

admiration admiración *f.*

advance: in —, de antemano

afraid: be — (of) tener (**7**) miedo (de), temer (—)

after *prep.* después de; *conj.* después (de) que

afternoon tarde *f.;* **good —,** buenas tardes; **in the —,** (*when hour is mentioned*) de la tarde, (*when hour is not mentioned*) por la tarde

again otra vez; **do something —,** volver (ue) (**78**) a hacer algo, hacer (**27**) algo otra vez

147

agosto *m.* August
agradable agreeable
agradecer (App. B, III, 2a) thank
agua *f.* water
aguador *m.* water seller
aguijonazo *m.* thrust
ahí there (*near person spoken to*)
ahora now
aire *m.* air, atmosphere
Albaicín *m. an old quarter of the
    city of Granada*
Alberto Albert
Alcalá *one of the main streets of
    Madrid*
Alcázar *m. royal palace of Moorish
    architecture in Seville*
alcornoque *m.* cork tree
aldea *f.* village
alegrarse (de) be glad
alegre joyful, happy
alegría *f.* joy, pleasure
alemán, –a German
Algeciras *town in southern Spain,
    near Gibraltar*
algo something
algodón *m.* cotton
alguacil *m.* bailiff
alguno, –a some; —a vez some-
    time, ever

Alhambra *f. old Moorish palace at
    Granada*
alma *f.* soul, heart
almuerzo *m.* lunch
alrededor (de) around, about
alto, –a tall, high
allá there
allí there
Amazonas *m. sing.* Amazon (*river
    in Brazil*)
ameno, –a pleasant
América *f.* America
americano, –a American
amigo, –a friendly; *noun* amigo
    m. friend (*male*), amiga *f.* friend
    (*female*);   querido —, dear
    friend; un — mío a friend of
    mine
amor *m.* love
andaluz, –a Andalusian
andar 54 go (*without definite des-
    tination*); — (+ *pres. part.*) be,
    keep (+ *pres. part.*)
andén *m.* platform
Andes *m. pl.* Andes (*mountain
    range in South America*)
animado, –a animated, lively
animal *m.* animal
anoche last night (evening)

---

ago: ten minutes —, hace diez
    minutos
agree estar (16) de acuerdo
Albert Alberto
Alhambra Alhambra *f.*
all todo, –a; — aboard! ¡ señores
    viajeros al tren! — that *rel.
    pron.* todo lo que; — (of) that
    demon. pron. todo eso (aquello)
allow permitir (—)
almost casi
along por
Alphonso Alfonso
Alphonso VI *king of Castile and
    Leon,* 1072–1109, *who captured
    Toledo,* 1085
already ya

also también
although aunque
always siempre
ambassador embajador *m.*
America América *f.*; North —
    (la) América del Norte; South
    —, (la) América del Sur
American americano, –a; — (*of
    U.S.A.*), norteamericano, –a;
    South —, sur(sud)americano, –a
amount to subir a, importar
amuse(oneself)divertir(se)(ie) 102
an un *m.*, una *f.*
and y, e (*before words beginning
    with* i *or* hi)
Andalusian andaluz, –a
another otro, –a

anteayer day before yesterday
antemano: de —, beforehand
antes (de) before (*time*); cuanto
  —, as soon as possible
antiguo, –a ancient, old
apenas scarcely, hardly
aplauso *m.* applause
aprender (a) learn
apunte *m.* note, annotation
aquel, –lla, –llos, –llas *adj.* that
aquél, –lla, aquello (*neut.*), –llos,
  –llas *pron.* that (one); the
  former
aquí here
árabe Arabic, Moorish
arabesco *m.* arabesque
árbol *m.* tree; — frutal fruit tree
arena *f.* sand
aritmética *f.* arithmetic; lección
  de —, arithmetic lesson
arquitectura *f.* architecture
arrastrar drag (away)
arrojarse (a) dash, dart
artículo *m.* article, thing

artista *m.* artist
artístico, –a artistic
asegurar assure
asir 173 seize
asistir be present
asunto *m.* subject, affair, business
atacar (App. B, III, 1) attack
ataque *m.* attack
atención *f.* attention
atento, –a attentive
Atlántico *m.* Atlantic
atraer 89 attract
atravesar (ie) 88 cross
aun (aún) even, yet
aunque although
autor *m.* author
aventurarse risk oneself, venture
¡ ay ! oh ! (*cry of surprise or pain*)
ayer yesterday
ayuda *f.* help, aid
ayudar (a) help, aid, assist
azucarillo *m. crisp, white, sponge-
like confection used to sweeten
water, chocolate, etc.*

Anthony Antonio; Saint —, San
  Antonio
any: —person alguna (cualquiera)
  persona; not — one (anybody)
  nadie, ninguno, –a (*with* no *before verb*); I have never seen
  anybody nunca he visto a nadie
anyhow en cualquier caso
anything: not —, nada (*with* no
  before verb); you never buy
  —, nunca compra Vd. nada
apartment habitación *f.*
appetite apetito *m.*   [III, 1)
approach acercarse (a) (App. B,
April abril *m.*
Aragon Aragón *m.*
arithmetical aritmético, –a
arrive (at) llegar (a) (App. B, III, 1)
art arte *f.*; fine —s bellas artes
as tan, como; — for en cuanto a;
  — large — tan grande como; —
  much (many) tanto, –a; — soon

— tan pronto como, luego que,
  así que; — soon — possible
  cuanto antes, tan pronto como
  posible
ashamed: be — (of) tener (7)
  vergüenza (de)
ask (*favor*) pedir (i) 114; (*question*) preguntar
asleep: fall —, dormirse 155
at en, a; — least al (a lo, por lo)
  menos; — night por la noche,
  de noche; — once en seguida, de
  una vez; — retail al por menor;
  — wholesale al por mayor;
  be — (*a place*) estar (16) en
Atlantic Atlántico *m.*
attention: pay — (to) prestar
  atención (a), hacer (27) caso (de)
August agosto *m.*
automobile automóvil *m.*
autumn otoño *m.*
away: go —, irse 53, marcharse

bahía *f.* bay
bailar dance
baile *m.* dance
bajar go down (stairs); get out
bajo under, beneath
Baltasar Carlos *son of Philip IV*
bandera *f.* flag
banderilla *f. small, gaily decorated
dart used in bullfighting*
banderillero *m. the one who sticks*

banderillas into the bull's neck
banquero *m.* banker
barato, –a cheap
Barcelona *seaport of Spain*
barranco *m.* ravine
barro *m.* clay
bastante enough, quite
beber drink
bebida *f.* drink
bello, –a beautiful

---

bad malo, –a; be — weather hacer
(27) mal tiempo
ball pelota *f.*
band cuadrilla *f.*
bank banco *m.*; (*of river*) orilla *f.*
basket cesta *f.*
bathe lavar
bathing place establecimiento (*m.*)
de baños
be ser 15, estar 16 (*for distinction
between* ser *and* estar *see* 13 *and*
14); — able poder (—) 66; —
acquainted with conocer 126;
— about to estar para; — afraid
(of) tener miedo (de), temer
(—); — a pity ser lástima; —
ashamed (of) tener vergüenza
(de); — at (*a place*) estar en;
— born nacer 126; — busy
ocuparse (en), emplearse (en);
— careful (to) tener cuidado
(de); — cold (*personal*) tener
frío, (*weather*) hacer (27) frío;
— contained caber 154; — delighted to tener mucho gusto
en; — dusty haber (6) polvo;
— fond of ser aficionado, –a
(a); — found hallarse, encontrarse (ue) 134; — (so) glad
(to) alegrarse (tanto) (de); —
very glad to tener mucho gusto
en; — good ser bueno, –a; —
good weather hacer (27) buen
tiempo; — homesick tener
nostalgia; — hungry tener hambre; — ill estar malo, –a (en-

fermo, –a); — in favor of estar
por; — long in tardar en;
— moonlight haber luna; —
necessary haber que, ser necesario (preciso) (—); — no
good no valer (144) nada (—);
— present asistir; — right
tener razón; — seasick marearse; — sleepy tener sueño;
— (very) sorry sentir (102)
(mucho); — thirsty tener sed;
— tired estar cansado, –a; —
warm (*personal*) tener calor;
(*weather*) hacer calor; — well
estar bueno, –a (bien); — worn
out no poder (66) más; —
worth (while) valer (144) (la
pena) (—); — wrong no tener
razón; — forty years old tener
cuarenta años; isn't it (so)?
¿ no es verdad ? ¿ verdad ?; her
eyes are blue ella tiene los ojos
azules; my eyes are tired tengo
los ojos cansados; your hands
are cold Vd. tiene las manos
frías; there is (are) hay; what
time is it ? ¿ qué hora es ?
beautiful hermoso, –a, bello, –a
because porque
bed cama *f.*; go to — acostarse 134
before (*time*) *prep.* antes de; *conj.*
antes (de) que; (*place*) delante de
beg pedir (i) (114) limosna
begin principiar (a), comenzar
(ie) (a) 88, empezar (ie) (a) 88
believe creer (App. B, II, 4)

Benavente, Jacinto *famous contemporary Spanish dramatist born in Madrid* 1866
biblioteca *f.* library
bien well
billete *m.* ticket; — **de ida y vuelta** round-trip ticket
blanco, –a white
Blasco Ibáñez, Vicente *famous contemporary Spanish novelist, native of Valencia, born* 1867
bondad *f.* goodness; **tenga Vd. la** — **(de)** please
bondadoso, –a kind
bonita, –a pretty, nice
bordado, –a embroidered
borde *m.* edge, border
brazo *m.* arm
bribón *m.* rascal, villain
bueno, –a good; **de** —**a gana** willingly
burro *m.* donkey, ass
buscar (App. **B, III,** 1) look for

caballero *m.* sir, gentleman
caballo *m.* horse; **a**—, on horseback
cabo *m.* end; **al** —, finally, at last
cada every, each
caer(se) **142** fall (down)
café *m.* café, restaurant
caja *f.* box
cajita *f.* little box
calcular calculate, reckon
calor *m.* heat; **hacer (27) (mucho)** —, be (very) warm (*weather*); **tener (7)** —, be warm (*personal*)
calle *f.* street
cambiar change
caminar walk, travel, go
camino *m.* road, way
campesino *m.* farmer, peasant
campo *m.* country, field
canción *f.* song
cansado, –a: **estar (16)** —, be tired
cantar sing
cantidad *f.* quantity, amount, number

---

best mejor
better mejor; **I like** —, me gusta más; — **late than never** más vale tarde que nunca
bill cuenta *f.*, factura *f.*
birthday cumpleaños *m.*
black negro, –a
blackboard pizarra *f.*, pizarrón *m.*, encerado *m.*
blue azul
boarding house casa (*f.*) de huéspedes
boat vapor *m.*, buque *m.*
bore aburrir
born: **be** —, nacer **126**
box caja *f.*
break quebrarse
breakfast desayuno *m.*
bridge puente *m.*
bright (*color*) vivo, –a
bring llevar, traer **89**
brother hermano *m.*; —(s) **and** sister(s) hermanos *m. pl.*

build edificar (App. **B, III,** 1) construír **172**
building edificio *m.*
bullfight corrida *f.* (de toros)
bullfighter torero *m.*
busy: **be** —, ocuparse (en), emplearse (en)
but pero, sino, sino que (*for distinction see* **36,** 2 *and* **36,** 2, footnote 3)
buy (of) comprar (a)
by por (*see* **112,** (6) *and* (7); de (*see* **133,** footnote 3); — **nine o'clock** para las nueve

café café *m.*
call llamar, gritar; **be** —**ed** llamarse
can (*be able*) poder (—) **66,** (*mental ability*) saber (—) **76;** — **endure (stand) no more** no poder más; — **not help** no poder menos de
candy dulce(s) *m.*

capa *f.* cape, cloak

capeador *m. bullfighter who attracts the attention of the bull by waving his cloak*

capilla *f.* chapel

capital *f.* capital (*city*)

Capitán Veneno *novel by Pedro A. de Alarcón, written* 1881

¡ caramba ! goodness !

Carlos Charles

carpintero *m.* carpenter

carta *f.* letter; — **en español** Spanish letter

casa *f.* house, home; — **de huéspedes** boarding house; **de — en —**, from house to house; **estar en —**, be at home; **ir a —**, go home

casi almost

casita *f.* little house, cottage

casta *f.* breed

castellano, –a Castilian

Castilla *f. Castile, old kingdom of Spain*

catedral *f.* cathedral

causa *f.* cause; **a — de** because of

celebrar celebrate, praise

céntimo $\frac{1}{100}$ of a peseta; **cinco —s** *equal about one cent*

centro *m.* center; **tener su — en** be centered in

cerca de near

cereza *f.* cherry

Cervantes, Miguel de (1547–1616) *author of* Don Quijote, *etc.*

cerveza *f.* beer

Cid, (el) Ruy Díaz de Bivar, *national hero of Spain, died* 1099

ciertamente certainly

cierto, –a certain

cima *f.* peak

cinco five

cincuenta fifty

ciudad *f.* city

civilización *f.* civilisation

clase *f.* class, kind

clásico, –a classic

clavar drive in, stick in

clima *m.* climate

---

cap gorra *f.*, gorro *m.*

capital (*city*) capital *f.*

captain capitán *m.*

car (*railroad*) vagón *m.*, coche *m.*

careful: be — (to) tener (**7**) cuidado (de)

careless descuidado, –a

carry llevar, traer **89**

cash hacer (**27**) efectivo, –a; **for —**, al contado; **pay — for** pagar (App. B, III, 1) al contado

castle castillo *m.*, fortaleza *f.*

catch coger (App. B, III, 2)

catholic católico, –a; **the — kings** (*king and queen*) los Reyes Católicos (*name applied to Ferdinand and Isabella*)

cave dwelling cueva *f.*

cent centavo *m.*

century siglo *m.*

certain cierto, –a

certainly ciertamente, sin duda

chair silla *f.*

chapter capítulo *m.*

Charles Carlos

Charles V *emperor of Germany, and king of Spain under the title of Charles I*

charming encantador, –a

cheap barato, –a

check cheque *m.*

cherry cereza *f.*

child niño *m.*, niña *f.*

chocolate chocolate *m.*

Christopher Cristóbal

church iglesia *f.*

cigar puro *m.*, habano *m.*, cigarro *m.*

city ciudad *f.*

civilization civilización *f.*

class clase *f.*; **Spanish —**, clase de español

clear claro, –a

climate clima *m.*

cloak abrigo *m.*

cojo, –a lame
colgar (ue) **134** (App. **B, III,** 1) hang
colombino, –a Columbian
Colón Columbus
color *m.* color
colorido *m.* coloring
columna *f.* column, pillar
combate *m.* combat
comedia *f.* comedy, play
comer eat
comercial commercial
comerciante *m.* merchant; — al por mayor wholesale merchant
comercio *m.* commerce
comida *f.* dinner, meal
como as, like
¿cómo? how? ¿— está Vd.? how are you?
compañero *m.* companion
compartimiento *m.* compartment
compensar compensate, reward
completamente completely
compra *f.* purchase
comprar buy; — a buy of
comprender understand
con with; — frenesí furiously; — mucho gusto with great pleasure, gladly; dar —, happen upon, meet, find

conducir **135** conduct, lead
confianza *f.* confidence
congelado, –a frozen
conmigo with me
conocer **126** know, be acquainted
conocido, –a (well) known
conocido *m.* acquaintance
conocimiento *m.* knowledge
consejo *m.* advice
consentir (en) **102** consent
considerar consider
consiguiente: por —, accordingly, consequently, therefore
construir **172** construct, build
contado: al — for cash; pagar al —, pay cash for
contar (ue) **134** count, relate, tell; — con rely (count) on
contemplar contemplate, behold
contener **7** contain
contenido *m.* contents
contento, –a glad, pleased
contestar answer
continente *m.* continent
contra against
conveniente suitable
convento *m.* convent
conversación *f.* conversation
copia *f.* copy
copiar copy

---

close cerrar (ie) **88;** the door —s la puerta se cierra
closed cerrado, –a
club club *m.*, círculo *m.*
coal carbón *m.*
coat (*sack coat*) americana *f.*
coffee café *m.*
coin moneda *f.*
cold frío, –a; have — hands tener las manos frías; be — (*weather*) hacer (**27**) frío, (*persons*) tener (**7**) frío
colloquially en lenguaje familiar
color color *m.*
Columbus Colón
come venir (a) **67;** — in entrar (en)

come! ¡vaya! — now! ¡pues vaya!
comfortable cómodo, –a
companion compañero *m.*
complain quejarse (de)
concerning en cuanto a, tocante a, respecto a (de)
conduct conducir **135**
conductor conductor *m.*, revisor *m.*
construct construir **172**
contents contenido *m.*
continually continuamente
contrast contraste *m.*
cool fresco, –a; be — (*weather*) hacer (**27**) fresco
cool (off) refrescarse (App. **B, III,** 1)

corbata *f.* necktie

Córdoba Cordoba (*city in southern Spain*)

correr run

corrida (de toros) *f.* bullfight

cosa *f.* thing; — de about, approximately

cosecha *f.* harvest

costa *f.* coast

creación *f,* creation

creer (App. B, III, 4) believe, think

crema *f.* cream

criado *m.* servant

Cristóbal Christopher

cuadrilla *f.* band, troop

cuadro *m.* picture, vegetable bed

cual, el, etc. which, who

¿ cuál ? which (one) ?

cualquier(a) any (one)

cuando when, whenever; de — (vez) en —, from time to time

cuanto, -a as much (many) (as); — antes as soon as possible; — más (menos) tanto más (menos) the more (less) the more (less); en — a as for, concerning

¿ cuánto, -a ? how much (*pl.* many) ? ¿ — tiempo how long ? ¿ — tiempo hace que llegó ? how long ago did he arrive ?

cuarenta forty

cuarto fourth; las siete menos

—, a quarter to seven o'clock

cuatro four; el — de julio July 4th

cubierto, -a covered

cubrir (Suppl. Ex. 1, C, VIII) cover

cuello *m.* neck

cuenta *f.* bill

cuidado *m.* care; tener — (de) be careful (of), take care (of)

cuidar (de) care (for), take care (of)

cumplir perform, carry out

cuyo, -a whose

chiste *m.* joke

dar 77 give; — con happen upon, meet

de of, from, by, to, in, as; than (*before affirmative numerals*); — antemano beforehand, in advance; — buena (mala) gana willingly (unwillingly); —lo que than; — noche at night; — ordinario ordinarily; — pronto suddenly; — propósito purposely; — repente suddenly; — veras in truth, truly, really

deber owe, ought; debe de estar he probably is, it is likely that he is

decidir (—), decidirse (a) decide

decir 28 say, tell; querer —, mean, signify

---

corner rincón *m.*

correct correcto, -a, exacto, -a bien; (*accounts*) conforme

cost costar (ue) 134

count contar (ue) 134

course: of — por supuesto

court (yard) patio *m.*; — of the Lions Patio de los Leones; pelota —, frontón *m.*

cousin primo *m.*, prima *f.*

cross atravesar (ie) 88

Cuban cubano, -a

cup taza *f.*

custom costumbre *f.*

dance baile *m.*

dance bailar

dancing baile *m.*

dare atreverse (a)

daughter hija *f.*

day día *m.*; — before yesterday antes de ayer, anteayer; every —, todos los días

deaf sordo, -a

deal: — with tratarse de; a great —, mucho

death muerte *f.*

December diciembre *m.*

decide decidir (—), decidirse (a)

dedicar (App. **B, III,** 1) dedicate, devote

dejar (—), leave, allow, let; — **de** fail, stop, cease

delante (de) in front (of)

delgado, –a slender

delicadísimo, –a very delicate

delicioso, –a delicious

dentro (de) within

dependiente *m.* clerk

desaparecer 126 disappear

desayunarse breakfast

desayuno *m.* breakfast

desconocido, –a unknown

describir (Suppl. Ex. 1, C, VIII) describe

descripción *f.* description

descubridor *m.* discoverer

descubrir (Suppl. Ex. 1, C, VIII) discover

desde from

desear (—) desire, wish

deseo *m.* desire

despacio slowly

despedirse (i) (de) **114** say good-bye, take leave (of)

después afterward; — **de** (*prep.*) after; — **que** (*conj.*) after;

poco — (de) soon after

día *m.* day; **todos los** —s every day

dicho *m.* saying

dichoso, –a fortunate, lucky

diestramente skillfully

diez ten

diferente different

difícil difficult

dificultad *f.* difficulty

digno, –a worthy

dinero *m.* money

dirección *f.* address

discípulo *m.* pupil, scholar

distintamente distinctly, clearly

distrito *m.* district, region

divertirse (ie) **116** amuse oneself, have a good time

doce twelve

don (*before given name of man*) Mr.

donde (**en** —) where, in which; **a** — (*with verbs of motion*) where, to which; —**quiera** wherever

¿ dónde? where? **¿ hasta** —? how far? [Mrs.

doña (*before given name of woman*)

dormir 155 sleep; —**se** fall asleep

dos two; — **veces** twice, two times

doscientos, –as two hundred

---

delay (in) tardar (en)

delighted: be — **to** tener (**7**) mucho gusto en

depot estación *f.*

desire desear (—), querer (—) **39**

dessert postre(s) *m.*

dictionary diccionario *m.*

die morir **125**

difficult difícil

dining room comedor *m.*

disagreeable desagradable

discover descubrir (Suppl. Ex. 1, C, VIII)

divide dividir; —**d by** dividido por

do hacer **27;** — **you not?** ¿ no es verdad? **it doesn't matter** no importa

doctor médico *m.*; (*used as a title*)

doctor *m.*

dog perro *m.*; **big** —, perro grande (*about two cents*); **little** —, perro chico (*about one cent*)

dollar peso *m.*, dólar *m.*

door puerta *f.*

doubt dudar

doubtless sin duda

downstairs: go — bajar

dozen docena *f.*; **five pesetas a** —, cinco pesetas la docena

draft letra *f.* (de cambio)

dress vestido *m.*, traje *m.*; **silk** —, vestido (traje) de seda

dress vestir (i) **116;** — **in** vestir de; — **oneself** vestirse

drink beber, tomar

drive (*automobile*) guiar

duda *f.* doubt
dudar (—) doubt
durante during
durar last

e and (*before word beginning with* i *or* hi)
ecuestre equestrian
echar throw; —se (a) throw oneself, rush; — de menos miss
Echegaray, José (1833–1916) *well-known Spanish dramatist, winner of Nobel prize for literature*
edad *f.* age, period
edición *f.* edition
edificar (App. **B, III,** 1) build
edificio *m.* building
efectivo, –a: hacer —, cash (*draft or check*)
ejemplo *m.* example
el (la, lo, los, las) the; — de that of; — que that, which; he (the one) who
embarcarse (App. **B, III,** 1) embark
embargo: sin — however, nevertheless
emoción *f.* emotion
empaquetar pack
empleado *m.* employee
en in, on, to, at, during; — casa at home; — cuanto a as for, concerning; — punto exactly; —

seguida at once, immediately; — vez (lugar) de instead of
encaje *m.* lace
encantador, –a charming
encantar charm, delight
encanto *m.* charm
encarnado, –a red
encontrar (ue) **134** meet, find: —se find oneself, be
enemigo *m.* enemy
enero *m.* January
enfermo, –a ill
engalanado, –a decorated
enredado, –a intertwined, involved
enseñar (a) show
ensueño *m.* dream
entender (ie) (App. **B, IV,** 1) understand
entero, –a entire
entonces then
entrada *f.* entrance; puerta de —, entrance door
entrar (a) (en *with noun or pron.*) enter, come in
entre among
entregar (App. **B, III,** 1) hand over, deliver
entusiasmar make enthusiastic
entusiasmo *m.* enthusiasm
entusiasta *m. & f.* enthusiast
enviar (a) send
épico, –a epic
época *f.* epoch, period, time

---

during durante
dusty: be — haber (**6**) polvo

each cada; — one cada uno, –a
early temprano, –a
easily fácilmente
eat comer, tomar
eating (el) comer
eight ocho; — o'clock las ocho; — hundred ochocientos, –as
eighty ochenta
either: nor I — ni yo tampoco
elegant: — society la alta sociedad

eleven once
elm olmo *m.*
employee empleado *m.*
endure: can — no more no poder (**66**) más
England Inglaterra *f.*
English(man) inglés *m.*; — lesson lección (*f.*) de inglés
enormous enorme
enough bastante, suficiente
enter entrar (a) (en *with noun or pron.*)
equal ser igual a

escaparate *m.* show window

escaparse escape, run away

escena *f.* scene

escenario *m.* stage

escoger (App. **B, III, 2**) choose; **se les escoge** they are chosen

Escorial, el *edifice built by Philip II, containing pantheon of Spanish kings, monastery, etc.*

escribir (Suppl. Ex. 1, **C, VIII**) write

escuchar (—) listen

escuela *f.* school

ese, –a, –os, –as *adj.* that

ése, –a, eso (*neut.*) **–os, –as,** *pron.* that (one); **por eso** therefore, accordingly, on that account

espada *f.* sword

España *f.* Spain

español, –a Spanish; **carta en —,** Spanish letter

especial special

espectáculo *m.* spectacle

esperanza *f.* hope, expectation

esperar (—) hope, expect

estación *f.* station (railroad); season (*of year*)

Estados Unidos *m. pl.* United States

estar 16 be; **— cansado, –a** be tired; **— de acuerdo** agree;

— de vuelta be back; **hace un año que estoy aquí** I have been here for a year

estatua *f.* statue

este, –a, –os, –as *adj.* this

éste, –a, esto (*neut.*) **–os, –as** *pron.* this (one); the latter

estocada *f.* stab, thrust, lunge

estoque *m.* rapier

estrecho, –a narrow

estudiante *m. & f.* student

estudiar study

Europa *f.* Europe

exactitud *f.* exactness, accuracy

excursión *f.* excursion

explorador *m.* explorer

exportar export

expresar express

extranjero, –a foreign; **al —,** abroad

extranjero *m.* foreigner

fábrica *f.* factory

fácil easy

fácilmente easily

factura *f.* bill, invoice

faja *f.* belt, sash

falta: hacer —, lack, be in want (need) of

familia *f.* family; **la vida de —,** family life

---

escape escapar(se)

Escorial el Escorial

especially sobre todo, especialmente

Europe Europa *f.*

even aun, (*after verb*) aún

evening noche *f.*; **last —,** anoche

ever alguna vez, jamás

every: — day todos los días

everybody todo el mundo·

everything todo

exactly (*time*) en punto; exactamente, precisamente

exceedingly muchísimo, sumamente, excesivamente

excellent excelente

exchange cambiar

excuse dispensar

exit salida *f.*

explain explicar (App. **B, III, 1**)

eye ojo *m.* **my —s are tired** tengo los ojos cansados; **her —** **are blue** ella tiene los ojos azules

face cara *f.*

fail: — to dejar de

fall caer **142; — asleep** dormirse **155**

famous famoso, –a

favor *m.* favor; **haga Vd. el — de** (+ *infin.*) please
favorable favorable
febrero *m.* February
felicitar congratulate
Felipe II Philip II (*king of Spain,* 1556–1598)
Fernando Ferdinand
fértil fertile
fielmente faithfully
figurilla *f.* statuette
Filadelfia Philadelphia
fin *m.* end; **a — de** (+ *infin.*) so as to; **a — de que** (+ *subj.*) so that; **a —es de** toward the end of; **al (por) —,** at last, finally
final final
flamenco, -a Flemish
flor *f.* flower
fonda *f.* inn
fotografía *f.* photograph
fraile *m.* friar, monk
frecuentar frequent
frenesí *m.* **con —,** furiously
fresa *f.* strawberry
fresco, -a cool; **hacer (27) —,** be cool (*weather*)
frío, -a cold; **hacer —,** be cold (*weather*)
frutal *adj.* fruit

fan abanico *m.*
fast de prisa, aprisa
fasten atar
father padre *m.* **— and mother** padres; **it is my —'s** es de mi padre
favor favor *m.*; **be in — of** estar (16) por
favorable favorable, propicio, -a
feel sentir (ie) **102; — like** tener (7) gana(s) de
Ferdinand Fernando
few pocos, -as; **a —** unos (pocos), unas (pocas), algunos, -as
fifteen quince; **— hundred** mil quinientos, -as
fifth quinto, -a
fifty cincuenta
finally al (por) fin
find hallar, encontrar (ue) **134; be** (*be found*) hallarse, encontrarse
fine: — arts bellas artes *f. pl.*
first primero, -a
five cinco; **— hundred** quinientos, -as
flee huír **172**
floor piso *m.*
flower flor *f.*
follow seguir **124**
fond: be —of ser aficionado, -a (a)
foot pie *m.*; **my feet are cold** tengo los pies fríos
football balompie *m.,* football *m.*
for para, por (*for distinction between* para *and* por *see* **112, 113**) **— a year I have been here** hace un año que estoy aquí; **— your sake** por Vd.; **as —,** en cuanto a; **be —** (*destined for*) **me (you)** ser para mí (Vd.)
foreign extranjero, -a
forget olvidar (—), olvidarse (de)
former aquél, -lla, -llos, -llas
forty cuarenta
four cuatro; **— hundred** cuatrocientos, -as
fourteen catorce
fourth: July —, el cuatro de julio
France Francia *f.*
Francis Francisco; **Saint —,** San Francisco
French francés, -a
frequent frecuente
frequently frecuentemente, con frecuencia
Friday viernes *m.*
friend amigo *m.,* amiga *f.*; **my —** (*direct address*) amigo mío
frog rana *f.*
from de, desde; **— time to time** de vez (cuando) en cuando
fruit fruta *f.*

fuente *f.* fountain
fuera outside, away
fuerte strong, powerful
fuertemente firmly
fumar smoke
función *f.* performance, show

gana *f.* desire, inclination; **de buena (mala) —,** willingly (unwillingly); **tener (7) gana(s) de** feel like, have a mind to
ganar earn
garrocha *f.* pike used in bullfighting
Gibraltar *British fortress at southern point of Spain*
Giralda *f. tower of the cathedral of Seville*
gitano, -a Gipsy
Goya, Francisco (1746-1828)

famous Spanish painter
gozar (de) enjoy
grabado *m.* illustration, picture
gracioso, -a gracious, pleasing
Granada *city in southern Spain, former capital of Moorish kings*
granadino, -a native of *or* coming from Granada
gran(de) large, big, great, grand
gritar cry out, shout, exclaim
grito *m.* shout, cry
grueso, -a thick, bulky
grupo *m.* group
Guadelevín *m. river in southern Spain*
guitarra *f.* guitar
gustar please; **me gusta más** I like (it pleases me) better
gusto *m.* pleasure; **tener (7) mucho — en** be very glad to

---

game juego *m.*
general general *m.*
gentleman señor *m.*
George Jorge
get obtener **7;** **— ready** prepararse (a); **— rid of** deshacerse (**27**) de; **— up** levántarse
Gipsy gitano, -a
Gipsy gitano *m.*, gitana *f.*
girl señorita *f.*, niña *f.* Gipsy **—** gitana *f.*
give dar **77**
glad alegre; be (so) **—** (to) alegrarse (tanto) (de); be very **—** to tener (**7**) mucho gusto en
gladly con mucho gusto
glass vaso *m.*; **—es** (*spectacles*) anteojos *m. pl.*, lentes *m. pl.*
gloomy triste, melancólico, -a
glove guante *m.*
go ir **53,** andar **54** (*not to definite destination*); **— away** irse, marcharse; **— down** (stairs) bajar; **— in** entrar(en); **— out** salir (de) **100;** **— to bed** acostarse **134;** **— to sleep** dormirse **155;**

— through pasar por; **— up** subir; **— with** acompañar, ir con; **let us —,** vamos
gold oro *m.*; it is **—,** es de oro
good bueno, -a; **— afternoon** buenas tardes; **— evening** (night) buenas noches; **— luck** fortuna *f.*, suerte *f.*, dicha *f.*; **— morning** buenos días; be **—,** ser bueno, -a; be no **—,** no valer (**144**) nada; have a **— time** divertirse (ie) **102**
goodbye adiós, hasta luego
goodness: my **—!** ¡ Diós mío !
gourd-shaped de la forma de una calabaza
gracefully graciosamente, con gracia
grain grano *m.*
Granada Granada *f.*; from **—,** granadino, -a
grasp asir **173**
great gran(de); a **— deal** mucho
greatly mucho
green verde
guide (*man*) guía *m.*; (*book*) guía *f.*

haber 6 have; — **polvo** be dusty; **hay** there is (are); **hay que** (+ *infin.*) it is necessary to; ¿ **qué hay que comer?** what is there to eat? **los (las) hay** there are some

habitación *f.* room, lodging, apartments

hablar speak, talk

hacer 27 make, do; — **buen (mal) tiempo** be good (bad) weather; — **(mucho) calor** be (very) warm (weather); — **(mucho) frío** be (very) cold (weather); — **falta** lack, be in want of; — **fresco** be cool (weather); —**se** become, be done; — **un viaje** take a trip; — **viento** be windy; ¿ **cuánto tiempo hace que llegó?** how long ago did he arrive? **hace un año** a year ago; **hace un año que llegó** he arrived a year ago; **hace un año que está aquí** he has been here for a year; **hacía un año que estaba aquí** he

had been here for a year; **haga Vd. el favor de** (+ *infin.*) please

hacia toward

hallar find; —**se** find oneself, be

hambre *f.* hunger; **tener (7) (mucha)** — be (very) hungry

haraposo, -a ragged

harina *f.* flour; **molino de** —, flour mill

hasta as far as, up to, until; ¿ — **dónde?** how far? — **que** until (*in clause*)

helado ice cream

herir (ie) 102 wound

hermana *f.* sister

hermanita *f.* little sister

hermano *m.* brother

hermoso, -a beautiful

hermosura *f.* beauty

héroe *m.* hero

herramienta *f.* tool

hijo *m.* son

historia *f.* history

histórico, -a historical

---

habit costumbre *f.*

half medio, -a; **at** — **past seven** a las siete y media

half mitad *f.* — **of the bill** la mitad de la cuenta

hall sala *f.*; — **of the Ambassadors** Sala de los Embajadores

hand mano *f.*; **my** —**s are cold** tengo las manos frías; **on the other** —, en cambio, por otra parte

handkerchief pañuelo *m.*; **linen** —, pañuelo de lino

happen suceder; — **upon** ·dar con

happily alegremente, felizmente

hard difícil

hat sombrero *m.*

have (*auxiliary*) haber **6**; (*possession*) tener **7**; — **to** (*necessity*) tener que; — **a good time** divertirse (ie) **102**; — **a headache** tener dolor de cabeza;

— **just** acabar de (+ *infin.*)

he él; — **who** el que, quien

head cabeza *f.*

headache dolor (*m.*) de cabeza; **have a** —, tener **(7)** dolor de cabeza

health salud *f.*

hear oír **143**

help ayudar (a) (*takes indirect object of the person*); **cannot** —, no poder (**66**) menos de

her *poss. adj.* su(s)

her *pron.* la, (*after Span. prep.*) ella

here aquí, (*after verbs of motion*) acá

hers *poss. pron.* el suyo, etc., el de ella, etc.

him le (lo), (*after Span. prep.*) él

his *poss. adj.* su(s)

his *poss. pron.* el suyo, etc., el de él, etc.; — **own** el suyo, etc., el propio, etc.

history historia *f.*

hombre *m.* man
hora *f.* hour, time; **¿ a qué —?** at
  what time?
hotel *m.* hotel
hoy today
huerta *f.* vegetable garden
huésped *m.* guest; **casa de —es**
  boarding house
huír **172** flee, run away

ida: **billete de — y vuelta** round-
  trip ticket
idea *f.* idea
idioma *m.* language
iglesia *f.* church
imaginar imagine
imaginario, **-a** imaginary
importancia *f.* importance
importante important

importar be of importance; **no
  importa** it does not matter
independencia *f.* independence
inglés, **-a** English
inmediatamente immediately, in-
  stantly
inscripción *f.* inscription
interés *m.* interest
interesante interesting
íntimo, **-a** intimate, private
invierno *m.* winter
ir **53** go; **—se** go away; **— estudiando** (*progressive construction*)
  be (keep) studying; **vamos** let
  us go **¡ vamos!** come! well!
Isabel Isabella
isla *f.* island
Italia *f.* Italy
italiano, **-a** Italian

---

home casa *f.*; **go —,** ir (**53**) a casa;
  be at —, estar (**16**) en casa
homesick: **be —,** tener (**7**) nostalgia
hope esperar (**—**)
horseback: **on —,** a caballo
hot caliente; **be —** .(*personal*)
  tener (**7**) calor, (*weather*) hacer
  (**27**) calor
hotel hotel *m.*
hour hora *f.*; **an — and a half** (una)
  hora y media
house casa *f.*
how? **¿** cómo? **— does one say?**
  ¿ cómo se dice? **— much** (many)
  ¿ cuánto, **-a? — old is he?**
  ¿ cuántos años tiene?
however sin embargo, no obstante
hundred (**one —**) cien(to); **five
  —,** quinientos, **-as**
hungry: **be —,** tener (**7**) hambre
hurry (up) apresurarse, darse (**77**)
  prisa
hurt lastimar, hacer (**27**) daño

I yo
ice cream helado *m.*; **strawberry**

—, helado de fresa
if si
ill enfermo, **-a,** malo, **-a**
imagine imaginarse, figurarse
important importante
impossible imposible
in en, de; (*after superlative*) de;
  — advance de antemano; **—
  order to** para (**+** *infin.*); **—
  regard to** en cuanto a; **— spite
  of** a pesar de; **— the morning**
  (*when hour is mentioned*) de la
  mañana, (*when hour is not
  mentioned*) por la mañana
infinitive infinitivo *m.*
inn fonda *f.*
insignificant insignificante
insist insistir (en), empeñarse (en)
instead of en vez (lugar) de
intend pensar (ie) (**—**) **88**
interesting interesante
into a, en
introduce presentar
irregular irregular
Isabella Isabel
Italian italiano, **-a**
its su(s)

jabón *m.* soap
jardín *m.* flower garden
joven *adj.* young
joven *m.* young man, *f.* young
  woman
jueves *m.* Thursday
juez *m.* judge
jugar **136** play
julio *m.* July
junio *m.* June
juventud *f.* youth

labrador *m.* laborer, farmer
labrar cultivate
lado *m.* side; **al otro —,** on the
  other side
lanza *f.* lance
lástima *f.* pity; **es —,** it is a pity;
  ¡ qué lástima! what a pity!
lateral lateral, at the side

lavarse wash oneself
lección *f.* lesson; **— de lectura
  (aritmética)** reading (arithmetic) lesson
lectura *f.* reading; **lección de —,**
  reading lesson
leer (App. **B, III, 4**) read
legumbres *f. pl.* vegetables
lejos far (away), distant; **a lo —,**
  in the (at a) distance
León: **Patio de los —es** *Court of
  the Lions in the Alhambra*
León *old kingdom in the north of
  Spain*
letra *f.* letter (*of alphabet*), hand-
  writing; **— (de cambio)** draft
levantar raise; **—se** rise, get up
libertad *f.* liberty
librería *f.* bookstore
libro *m.* book

January enero *m.*
John Juan
Joseph Yusuf (*Moorish word for
  Spanish* José)
July julio *m.*
June junio *m.*
just: have **—,** acabar de (+ *infin.*)

keep (*sign of progressive construction*); **they — studying** están
  estudiando
key llave *f.*
kilometer kilómetro *m.*
king rey *m.,* **the Catholic Kings**
  (*King and Queen*) los Reyes
  Católicos
know saber **76;** conocer **126; —
  how to** saber **(—)** (+ *infin.*);
  — each other conocerse; (*for
  discussion of* **saber, conocer** *and*
  poder *see* **76,** footnote 1)

lace encaje *m.*
lack hacer (**27**) falta a, faltar a;
  I — it me (hace) falta
lady señora *f.*

lame cojo, –a; **the — man** el cojo
landlady patrona *f.*
language idioma *m.,* lengua *f.*
lantern linterna *f.*
large gran(de)
last pasado, –a; **— night (evening)** anoche; **—week** la semana
  pasada
late tarde; **better — than never**
  más vale tarde que nunca
latter éste, –a, –os, –as
laugh (at) reírse (i) (de) **101**
lazy perezoso, –a, holgazán, –a,
  haragán, –a
learn aprender **(—)**
least: at **—,** al (a lo, por lo) menos
leave salir (a) (*takes prep.* de
  before noun or pron.) **100**
less menos; **the — the more**
  cuanto menos tanto más
lesson lección *f.;* **English —,** lección de inglés
let dejar **(—),** permitir **(—); —
  us go** vamos, vámonos
liberty libertad *f.*
library biblioteca *f.*

lidia *f.* fight, bullfight
lidiador *m.* fighter
limosna *f.* alms, charity
limosnita *f.* little gift
lindo, -a pretty, nice, fine
listo, -a ready
literatura *f.* literature
lo the (*neut.*); a — lejos in the
(at a) distance; por — tanto
accordingly, therefore; todo —
nuevo everything new
lograr (—) succeed (in), obtain
Lope de Vega (1562–1635) *famous
Spanish dramatist*
Lucía Lucy
lucha *f.* struggle, fight
Luis Louis

llamar call; ¿ cómo se llama esto ?
what is the name of this ?
llave *f.* key
llegada *f.* arrival
llegar (App. B, III, 1a) arrive (at),
reach; —se a approach
llevar carry, bring; —se take
away
lluvia *f.* rain

madre *f.* mother
Madrid *f. capital of Spain*
madrileño, -a native of *or* coming
from Madrid
maestra *f.* teacher; obra —,
masterpiece
maestro *m.* teacher, schoolmaster
magnífico, -a magnificent, fine,
splendid
malo, -a sick, bad; estar (16) —,
be sick; ser (15) —, be bad
mancha *f.* spot, stain
mano *f.* hand
manuscrito *m.* manuscript
mañana *f.* morning; pasado —, day
after to-morrow; por la —, in the
morning (*hour not mentioned*),
de la — (*hour mentioned*)
mapa *m.* map
mar *m.* sea
maravilla *f.* marvel
maravilloso, -a marvelous, wonderful
marcharse go away, depart
marearse be seasick
marginal marginal
marido *m.* husband

lie: — down acostarse (ue) 134
lieutenant teniente *m.*
life vida *f.*
like gustar a; I — (better) me
gusta (más); I should — to
quisiera (—), me gustaría (—)
like *adv.* como; feel —, tener (7)
gana(s) de
likewise también, asimismo
linen lino *m.*
lion león *m.*, *see* patio
list lista *f.*
listen! ¡ oiga !
little *adj.* pequeño, -a, chico, -a;
a — while un rato
little *adv.* poco; — by —, poco a
poco; a —, un poco
live vivir
lively vivo, -a, animado, -a

long: a — while mucho tiempo;
be (so) — in tardar (tanto) en;
for a — time I have been looking for you hace mucho (tiempo)
que le busco a Vd.
look for buscar (App. B, III, C, 1)
loudly alto, fuerte
Louis Luis
luck (*good luck*) fortuna *f.* dicha *f.*

magnificent magnífico, -a
make hacer 27; — acquaintance
conocer 126
man hombre *m.*
many muchos, -as; as — as
tantos (-as) como; how —?
¿ cuántos? -as?
map mapa *m.*
market mercado *m.*

martes *m.* Tuesday

marzo *m.* March

más more (*sign of comparative*); most (*sign of superlative*); — de (+ *numerals*) more than; poco — o menos about, approximately

matador *m. bullfighter who kills the bull with a rapier*

mayor older, greater; greatest, chief; al por —, (at) wholesale

medio, -a half; las siete y media half past seven o'clock

mejor better, best

menor younger; al por —,(at) retail

menos less; al (a lo, por lo) —, at least; no poder (66) — de do no less than, cannot help; poco más o —, about, approximately

menudo: a —, often

mercado *m.* market

meridional southern

mes *m.* month

mesa *f.* table

mesita *f.* little table

metro *m.* meter

mezquita *f.* mosque

miedo *m.* fear; por — de que for fear that; tener (7) —, be afraid

mientras (que) while; — tanto meanwhile

miércoles *m.* Wednesday

mil thousand

mío, -a my, of mine; un amigo —, a friend of mine

mirar look (at)

mismo, -a same, self; yo —, myself

mitad *f.* half

modelo *m.* model

moderno, -a modern

modo *m.* manner, way

Mohámed V *king of Granada*

molino *m.* mill; — de harina flour mill

momento *m.* moment

monasterio *m.* monastery

montaña *f.* mountain

monumento *m.* monument

morir (ue) **125** die

moro, -a Moorish

moro *m.* Moor

Martin Martín

Mary María

mathematician matemático *m.*

matter: it does not —, no importa; what is the — with you? ¿ qué tiene Vd. ? ¿ qué le pasa a Vd. ?

May mayo *m.*

me me; to —, me

meal comida *f.*

mean querer (**39**) decir

meanwhile entretanto, mientras tanto

Mediterranean Mediterráneo *m.*

meeting sesión *f.*, reunión *f.*,

Mexican mejicano, -a

mine mina *f.*, silver —, mina de plata

mine *pron.* el mío, etc.

minus menos

minute minuto *m.*; ten —s ago

hace diez minutos

mirror espejo *m.*

Miss señorita, Srta.

miss echar de menos

mistake error *m.*, equivocación *f.*

moderate módico, -a

Mohamed Mohámed

Monday lunes *m.*

money dinero *m.*

month mes *m.*

moonlight luz (*f.*) de la luna; be —, haber (6) luna

more más; —than (*before numerals in affirmative*) más de; can endure no —, no poder (66) más; the — the —, cuanto más tanto más

morning mañana *f.*; good — buenos días; in the — (*when hour is mentioned*) de la mañana, (*when hour is not mentioned*) por la mañana

mostrar (ue) **134** show; se me
mostró I was shown

mozo *m.* boy, waiter

mucho, –a much, very great, *pl.*
many; tener **(7)** hacer **(27)** — frió,
calor, etc. be very cold, warm, etc.

mucho *adv.* much, very much, a
great deal; muchísimo very much

muerto, –a dead, killed

mujer *f.* woman

mula *f.* mule

muleta *f. red flag used by matadors*

multiplicar (App. B, III, 1) multi-
ply

mundo *m.* world

muralla *f.* wall, rampart

Murillo   (1617–1682)   *Spanish
painter*

museo *m.* museum; — del Prado
Prado Museum (*National Museum of painting and sculpture*)

música *f.* music

músico *m.* musician

muy very; — señora mía dear
Madam

nacional national

nada nothing, not anything; —
que hacer nothing to do

nadie nobody, no one, not any one

natal native

natural natural, native

naturalmente naturally

necesario, –a necessary

necesitar (—) need

negro, –a black

nieve *f.* snow

ninguno, –a no one, none, not any

niña *f.* girl

niño *m.* boy, child

no no, not

noche *f.* night; por la —, in the
evening, at night; de —, at
night

nombre *m.* name

noroeste *m.* northwest

---

most (of) la mayor parte de, los
más de

mother madre *f.*

movies cínema *m.*, cine m.

Mr. señor, Sr.

Mrs. señora, Sra.

much mucho, –a; as — as
tanto(a) como; so —, tanto, –a;
very —, mucho, muchísimo

museum museo *m.*

must tener **(7)** que

my mi(s); — friend (*direct address*)
amigo mío; — goodness! ¡Diós
mío!

myself yo mismo, –a

name nombre *m.*, the — of this is
esto se llama; what is the —
of? ¿cómo se llama ?

national nacional

near cerca de

necessary necesario, –a; it is —,
hay que, es necesario (preciso)

necktie corbata *f.*

never nunca, jamás (*with no before
verb*); better late than —, más
vale tarde que nunca

nevertheless no obstante, sin embargo

New York Nueva York

newspaper periódico *m.*

next próximo, –a, que viene

night noche *f.*; at —, por la noche,
de noche; last —, anoche

night-watchman sereno *m.*

nine nueve; — hundred novecientos, –as

nineteen diez y nueve, diecinueve

ninety noventa

no no; — one nadie, ninguno, –a
(*with no before verb*); be — good
no valer **(144)** nada

nobody nadie (*with no before verb*)

noise ruido *m.*

none, ninguno, –a (*with no before verb*)

noon mediodía *m.*

norteamericano, –a American (*of U.S.A.*)
novela *f.* novel
Nueva York New York
nueve nine
nuevo, –a new; todo lo —, everything new
nunca never (*with* no *before verb*)

o or
obra *f.* work; — maestra masterpiece
obtener 7 obtain
ocuparse(en) occupy(busy) oneself
ocho eight
ochocientos, –as eight hundred
ofrecer 126 offer
oír 143 hear, listen
¡ ojalá ! would that
oler 174 smell

olivo *m.* olive tree
olvidar (—), —se (de) forget
once eleven
oportunidad *f.* opportunity
oratorio *m.* oratory
ordinario, –a ordinary; de —, ordinarily
oro *m.* gold
otro, –a other, another; al — lado on the other side

Pacífico *m.* Pacific
padre *m.* father; *pl.* parents
pagar (App. B, III, 1) pay
país *m.* country
paisaje *m.* landscape
palabra *f.* word
palacio *m.* palace
palco *m.* box
palma *f.* palm tree

nor ni; — I either ni yo tampoco
North America la América del Norte
northern el norte de
not no; — any ninguno, –a; do you —? ¿ no es verdad ? ¿ verdad ?
nothing nada (*with* no *before verb*)
now ahora

object objeto *m.*, artículo *m.*, cosa *f.*
obtain obtener 7, lograr (—)
o'clock: it is one —, es la una; it is half past two —, son las dos y media
of de; — course por supuesto
office oficina *f.*, despacho *m.*
often a menudo, muchas veces
oh! ¡ oh!
old viejo, –a; be forty years —, tener (7) cuarenta años; how — is he? ¿ cuántos años tiene ?
older mayor
on en, sobre, encima de; — horseback a caballo; — January 2nd el dos de enero; — Monday el lunes

once una vez; at —, en seguida, de una vez
one uno, –a; no — ninguno, –a, nadie (*with* no *before verb*); the — which el que, etc.
only sólo, solamente, no . . . sino, no más que
open abrir (Suppl. Ex. 1, C, VIII)
open abierto, –a
opportunity oportunidad *f.*
or o
orange naranja *f.*
order mandar (—), ordenar (—); in — to para (+ *infin.*)
other otro, –a; on the — hand en cambio, por otra parte
ought deber (—)
our nuestro, –a
ours el nuestro, etc.
overcoat sobretodo *m.*
owe deber
own propio, –a; his —, el propio

pack empaquetar, (*trunk*) hacer 27
package paquete *m.*
page página *f.*

panorama *m.* panorama, view
Panteón, Pantheon, burial vault
pañuelo *m.* handkerchief
papel *m.* paper
paquete *m.* package, bundle
para to, in order to, for
Pardo, el *royal castle near Madrid*
parecer **126** appear, seem
parte *f.* part
pasado: — mañana day after
  tomorrow
pasajero *m.* traveler, passenger
pasar (a) pass, spend; — por
  cross over
pase *m.* thrust
pasear(se) take a walk
paseo *m.* promenade, walk
pasmoso, –a amazing, wonderful
patio *m. inner courtyard*; — de
  los Leones Court of the Lions
patria *f.* fatherland, native country
patrona *f.* landlady
pedir (i) **114** ask (*favor*), request
pena *f.* trouble; valer (**144**) la —,
  be worth while
penetrar penetrate

pensar (ie) **88** think; (—) intend;
  (en) think about (of)
peñón *m.* cliff, large rock
pequeño, –a little, small
perder (ie) (App. **B, IV, 1**) lose
periódico *m.* newspaper
permanecer **126** remain
permiso *m.* permission
permitir (—) permit
pero but
perseguir **124** pursue
personalmente personally
pesado, –a heavy
pesar: a — de in spite of
picador *m. horseman in a bullfight
  who fights with a pike*
picar (App. **B, III, 1**) thrust (at)
pieza *f.* play
pintar paint, depict
pintor *m.* painter
pintoresco, –a picturesque
pintura *f.* painting
plata *f.* silver
plaza *f.* square; — de toros bullring
pleito *m.* lawsuit

---

paragraph párrafo *m.*
park parque *m.*
part parte *f.*
pass pasar (a)
passerby transeunte
past: at half — seven a las siete
  y media
patience paciencia *f.*
pay pagar (App. B, III, 1) — attention to prestar atención a, hacer
  caso de; — cash pagar al contado
pear pera *f.*
pelota pelota *f.*, — court frontón *m.*
pencil lápiz *m.*
penknife cortaplumas *m.*
people gente *f.*; many —, mucha
  gente
permission permiso *m.*
permit permitir (—)
person persona *f.*; any —, al-

guién, alguna persona
Peru el Perú
peseta peseta *f.* (*Spanish coin
  worth normally twenty cents*)
Philip Felipe
picnic partida (*f.*) de campo
picture cuadro *m.*
pin alfiler *m.*
pity lástima *f.*; it is a —, es lástima; what a —! ¡ qué lástima!
play pieza *f.*, comedia *f.*, drama
  m.; (*performance*) función *f.*
play jugar **136**; —pelota jugar
  a la pelota; it is —ed se juega
player jugador *m.*
please gustar a (uno); haga Vd.
  el favor de, tenga Vd. la bondad
  de, sírvase Vd. (—); it —s me
  (greatly) me gusta (mucho)
pleasure gusto *m.*, placer *m.*

pluma *f.* pen
pobre poor
poco *adv.* little; — **a** —, little by little; — **después** a little later, soon after; — **más o menos** about, approximately
poder 66 be able, can; **no — más** not be able to endure more; **no — menos de** do no less than, cannot help
político, -a political
polvo *m.* dust; **haber (6) (mucho)** —, be (very) dusty
poner 40 put, offer; **—se (a)** begin
por for, through, by, on, over, in, to, along, per; — **consiguiente (eso, lo tanto)**, consequently, therefore, accordingly; — **fin** finally; — **la mañana (noche)** in the morning (evening); — (+ *adj. or adv.*) **que** however; — **miedo de que** for fear that; — **supuesto** of course; **al — mayor** (at) wholesale; **al — menor** (at) retail; **pasar —** cross over
¿ por qué ? why
porque because
posible possible
Prado *m. boulevard in Madrid on which is the Museo del Prado*
precio *m.* price

preciso, -a necessary, required; **ser —**, be necessary
pregunta *f.* question
preguntar ask (*question*)
presentar present, introduce
presidente *m.* president, presiding officer
prestar lend; — **atención a** pay attention to
primero, -a first
príncipe *m.* prince
principiar (a) begin
principio *m.* beginning
probabilidad *f.* probability
probar (ue) 134 prove
profesor *m.* professor
promesa *f.* promise
prometer (—) promise
pronto soon; **de —**, suddenly
propio, -a own
proponer 40 propose
propósito: de —, purposely
próximo, -a next
pueblo *m.* town, village, people
puente *m. & f.* bridge
puerta *f.* door; — **de entrada** entrance door
puerto *m.* port
pues for, since; well; — **sí** why yes, yes indeed; — **bien** well then
puesto que since

---

plus más, y
pocket bolsillo *m.*
poet poeta *m.*
pond charco *m.*, alberca *f.*
poor pobre; **the — man** el pobre
Portuguese portugués, -a
possible posible; **as soon as —**, cuanto antes, tan pronto como posible
possibly (*for discussion of future and conditional of possibility see* **45**)
postcard tarjeta (*f.*) postal
pound libra *f.*
prefer preferir (ie) **102** gustar

más a (uno)
president presidente *m.*
pretty bonito, -a, lindo, -a
price precio *m.*; **wholesale —**, precio al por mayor
probable probable
probably probablemente (*for discussion of future and conditional of probability see* **45**)
problem problema *m.*
professor profesor *m.*
promise prometer (—)
proverb dicho *m.*, refrán *m.*
provided: — that con tal que
province provincia *f.*

punto *m.* point; **en** — exactly

que *conj.* that, than; **de lo** —, than
que (**el que**, etc.) *pron.* who, which, that; **lo** —, that which, what, which
¿ qué ? what ?
¡ qué ! what (a) !
quebrar break
quedar(se) remain, be
queja *f.* complaint
quejarse (de) complain
querer (—) **39** wish, desire, want; — **decir 28** mean; (donde-quiera wherever)
querido dear
quien who, the one who; **a** — (to) whom; **de** —, of whom, whose
¿ quién ? who ? ¿ **a**—? (to) whom ?
Quijote, Don *famous book of Cervantes published* 1604
quince fifteen
Quintero, Serafín *and* Joaquín *contemporary dramatists, born in* 1871 *and* 1873, *respectively*
quinto, –a fifth
quitar (a) take away (from)

Rafael Raphael (*celebrated Italian painter,* 1483–1520)
rato *m.* short time, little while
razón *f.* reason; **tener (6)** —, be right
real royal
recibir receive, meet, welcome
recordar (ue) **134** remember, remind
recuerdo *m.* souvenir; **con muchos** —s with best regards
redondel *m.* arena (*of bullring*)
redondo, –a round
regar (App. **B, III, 1**) irrigate
región *f.* region
regresar return
reina *f.* queen
reinado *m.* reign
reino *m.* kingdom
reír(se) (de) **101** laugh (at)
rendirse surrender
repente: **de** —, suddenly
repetir (i) **114** repeat
representar represent
respetar respect
responder respond, reply
retrato *m.* picture, portrait
reunirse meet
rey *m.* king; *pl.* kings, king and queen

---

purposely de propósito
put (on) poner **40**
Pyrenees los Pirineos

quarter cuarto *m.*; **at a** — after five a las cinco y cuarto
queen reina *f.*
question pregunta *f.*, cuestión *f.* it is a — of se trata de
quickly aprisa, de prisa, rápidamente, prontamente

ragged haraposo, –a
railroad ferrocarril *m.*; **by** —, por ferrocarril
rain lluvia *f.*
rapidly rápidamente
reach llegar a (App. **B, III, C, 1**)
read leer (App. **B, III, 4**)
ready listo, –a; **get** —, prepararse
realize darse (**77**) cuenta (de), hacerse cargo (de)
receive recibir
recognize reconocer **126**
red rojo, –a, colorado, –a
regard: **in** — **to** en cuanto a
reign reinado *m.*
remain quedar(se)
remedy remedio *m.*
remember acordarse (ue) (de) **134,** recordar (ue) (—) **134**
rent alquilar
retail: **at** — al por menor
return volver (ue) (a) **78**

ricamente richly
rico, –a rich
río *m.* river
Rioja *district in northern Spain*
Roberto Robert
rodear go around
rogar (ue) **134** request, beg, entreat
romántico, –a romantic
Ronda *city in southern Spain*
Rubens, Peter Paul *Flemish painter*

S. S. S. = su **seguro servidor**
your humble servant
saber (—) **76** know (how)
sala *f.* hall, parlor; — de los Embajadores Hall of the Ambassadors
salida *f.* departure, appearance
salir (a) **144** go (come) out, leave
saltar jump, leap
salud *f.* health
saludar greet, speak to
sangre *f.* blood
Sangre y Arena *novel of Blasco
Ibáñez, dealing with bullfighting*
San Lorenzo St. Lawrence
sarcófago *m.* tomb
sed *f.* thirst; **tener** (**7**) (**mucha**)
—, be (very) thirsty

seda *f.* silk
seguida: en —, at once
seguir 124 follow
segundo, –a second
seguramente surely, certainly
seguro, –a sure, certain; **S. S. S.**
= su — **servidor** your humble
servant
seis six
semana *f.* week
semejante similar
sendero *m.* path
sentado, –a seated, sitting
sentarse (ie) **88** sit down
sentencia *f.* sentence, decision
sentir (ie) **102** feel, regret
señor sir, gentleman, Mr.
señora lady, Mrs.; **muy — mía**
dear Madam
septiembre *m.* September
ser 15 be; — **aficionado a** be fond
of; — **necesario** (**preciso**) be
necessary; **es lástima** (**verdad**)
it is a pity (true); **son las nueve**
it is nine o'clock; **serán** (**serían**) **las nueve** it is (was)
probably nine o'clock
sereno *m.* night-watchman

---

rich rico, –a; **exceedingly** —,
riquísimo, –a
rid: get — **of** deshacerse (**27**) de
right derecho, –a; **be** —, tener
river río *m.*   [razón
road camino *m.*
Robert Roberto
rock piedra *f.*
Rome Roma *f.*
room cuarto *m.*, habitación *f.*
round redondo, –a
royal real; — **Theater** Teatro Real
ruin echar a perder

saint santo *m.*, santa *f.*; —
Anthony San Antonio; — **Fran-
cis** San Francisco· — **Sebastian**
San Sebastián

sake: for your —, por Vd.
same mismo, –a; **at the** — **time**
a la vez, al mismo tiempo
sand-fly mosca (*f.*) de los arenales
satisfied satisfecho, –a, contento,
Saturday sábado *m.*   [–a
save ahorrar
say decir **28**; **it is said** (**one** —s)
se dice
school escuela *f.*
seasick: be — marearse
seated sentado, –a
Sebastian Sebastián; **Saint** —
San Sebastián
second segundo, –a
see ver **87**; — **again** volver (**78**) a
ver; **you were** —n se le vió a Vd.
send enviar (App. **B**, III, 3)

servidor *m.* servant; S. S. S. *or* su seguro —, your humble servant

servir (i) **115** serve, use; — de serve as; —se be used; ¿ para (de) qué sirve ? of what use is it ?

sesenta sixty

sesión *f.* session

Sevilla Seville (*city in southwest Spain*)

sevillano, –a Sevillian

si if, whether

sí yes

siempre always

sierra *f.* ridge of mountains

Sierra Nevada *range of mountains in southern Spain*

siete seven

siglo *m.* century; hace un — que it is a century ago that

siguiente following

silencio *m.* silence

silla *f.* chair

sin (que) without; — embargo however, nevertheless

sincero, –a sincere

singular, singular, peculiar

sino (que) but (*see* **36,** 2 *and* **36,** 2, *footnote* 3)

sobre over, upon, on, about, concerning; — todo above all, especially

sobrevenir **67** take place, occur

solemnidad *f.* solemnity

soler (ue) (—) **78** be accustomed to

solo, –a alone

sonido *m.* sound

sorprendente surprising

sorpresa *f.* surprise

---

serve servir (i) **115**

seven siete; at half past — o'clock a las siete y media; at ten minutes to —, a las siete menos diez

several varios, –as, algunos, –as

shave afeitarse

shine: the sun is shining hay (hace) sol

shop tienda *f.*

show mostrar (ue) **134,** enseñar (a); you were —n se le mostró

show función *f.*; vaudeville —, función de variedades

silk seda *f.*; — dress vestido (traje) de seda

silver plata *f.*; — mine mina de plata

since desde (que), (*causal*) puesto que; — then he has (had) been there desde entonces está (estaba) allí

sing cantar

singing (el) cantar

sir señor *m.*, caballero *m.*

sister hermana *f.*; brother(s) and sister(s) hermanos *m. pl.*

sit: — down sentarse (ie) **88**

six seis

sixteen diez y seis, dieciséis

sixty sesenta

sky cielo *m.*

sleep: go to —, dormirse **155**

sleepy: be —, tener (7) sueño

slowly despacio

small pequeño, –a

smell oler **174;** — good oler bien

so tan, así, lo; — much tanto, –a; — that para que, a fin de que, de modo (manera) que

society sociedad *f.*; elegant — la alta sociedad

some unos, –as, algunos, –as; — one alguién, alguno, –a

something alguna cosa, algo

sometimes algunas veces

somewhere en alguna parte

song canción *f.*

soon pronto; as — as tan pronto como, luego que, así que; as — as possible cuanto antes, tan pronto como posible

sorry: be (very) — sentir (ie) **102** (muchio); be — for it sentirlo

su(s) his, her, your (*formal*), their
subido, −a high (*price*)
subir(a) go up, climb; (*train*) get on
súbito, −a sudden
suceder happen
suelo *m.* ground
suerte *f.* fate; (*good*) luck; feature (*in bullfighting*), "stunt"
sumar add
suponer **40** suppose
supuesto: por —, of course
sur *m.* south; el — de southern
suspiro *m.* sigh
suyo, −a *adj.* his, her, your (*formal*), its, their
suyo (el —, etc.) *pron.* his, hers,
yours (*formal*), its, theirs

tal such (a)
también also, likewise, besides
tampoco neither
tan *adv.* as, so
tanto, −a so (as) much; *pl.* so (as) many; cuanto más — más the more the more; por lo — accordingly, therefore; tener (**7**) — cuidado be so careful
tardar en be long in, delay in
tarde late
tarde *f.* afternoon; por la —, in the afternoon
tarjeta *f.* (de visita) calling card

south sur *m.* sud *m.*
South America la América del Sur
South American sur(sud)americano, −a
southern meridional, el sur de
souvenir recuerdo *m.*
Spain España *f.*
Spaniard español *m.*, española *f.*
Spanish español, −a, castellano, −a; — class clase (*f.*) de español; — Rome la Roma de España
speak hablar
spite: in — of a pesar de
spring primavera *f.*
staff palo *m.*
stand: not — more no poder más
star estrella *f.*
station estación *f.*
statue estatua *f.*
stay quedar(se) (a)
steamer vapor *m.*
still todavía, aun, (*after verb*) aún
stop dejar de
story historia *f.*, cuento *m.*
strawberry fresa *f.*; — ice cream helado de fresa
street calle *f.*
streetcar tranvía *m.*
strength fuerza *f.*
strike dar (**77**) contra

strong fuerte
student estudiante *m. & f.*; alumno *m.*, alumna *f.*
study estudiar
studying (el) estudiar
subjunctive subjuntivo *m.*
such (a) tal
suddenly de repente
sufficient suficiente, bastante
sugar azúcar *m.*
suit vestido *m.*
suitcase maleta *f.*
sum suma *f.*
summer verano *m.*
sun sol *m.*; the — is shining hay (hace) sol
Sunday domingo *m.*
sunny: be (very) —, hacer (mucho) sol
swim nadar

table mesa *f.*
Tagus Tajo *m.*
take tomar; — a walk dar un paseo, pasear(se), ir a paseo
tale cuento *m.*
talk hablar
talkative hablador, −a
tall alto, −a, grande
taxi taxímetro *m.*

teatro *m.* theater
tela *f.* cloth
temer (—) fear
temprano early
tener **7** have; — (**mucho**) calor
be (very) warm; — **cuidado**
(**de**) be careful (of); — **gana(s)**
de feel like, have a mind to;
—**hambre** be hungry; —**miedo**
(**de**) be afraid (of); — **mucho**
gusto en be very glad to; —
que have to, must; — **razón** be
right; — **sed** be thirsty; **tenga**

Vd. la bondad de please
tercero, –a third
terminar (en) end, finish
tertulia *f.* evening party
terreno *m.* land, field
Ticiano Titian (*Italian painter*)
tiempo *m.* time, weather; ¿ cuánto
— **hace que vino ?** how long ago
did he come ? **hacer** (**27**) **buen**
(**mal**) —, be good (bad) weather
tienda *f.* shop, store; — **al por**
menor retail store
tierra *f.* land, country

---

tea te *m.*
teacher maestro *m.*, maestra *f.*,
profesor *m.*
tear out romper (Suppl. Ex. 1, **C**,
VIII), sacar, arrancar (App. **B**,
tell decir **28** [III, 1)
ten diez; — **hundred** mil
tenth décimo, –a
than que, de, de lo que, de (+ *def.*
art.) que (*for discussion see* **84**)
thanks (thank you) gracias
that *adj.* (*near person spoken to*)
ese, –a, –os, –as; (*remote from*
speaker and person spoken to)
aquel, –lla, –llos, –llas
that (one) *pron.* (*near person*
spoken to) ése, –a, –o (*neut.*),
–os, –as; (*remote from speaker*
and person spoken to) aquél,
–lla, –llo (*neut.*) –llos, —llas;
all (of) —, todo eso (aquello)
that *conj.* que
the el, la, lo (*neut.*), los, las
theater teatro *m.*
them los, las, (*after Spanish prep.*)
ellos, ellas; **to** —, les
themselves ellos mismos, ellas
mismas, (*after Spanish prep.*) sí;
(*object of verb*) se
then entonces
there allí, (*after verb of motion*)
allá; — **is** (**are**) hay
therefore por lo tanto, por eso

thing cosa *f.* artículo *m.*
think pensar (ie) **88**, (*believe*) creer
(App. **B**, III, 4); — **of** (*turn*
attention to) pensar en
third tercero, –a
thirsty: be —, tener (**7**) sed
thirteen trece
thirty treinta
this *adj.* este, –a, –os, –as
this (one) *pron.*, éste, –a, –o (*neut.*)
–os, –as; those of los (las) de;
those who (which) los (las) que
thousand mil; one (a)—, mil
three tres
through por
throw echar, tirar, lánzar
Thursday jueves *m.*
thus así, de este (ese) modo
ticket billete *m.*
tie corbata *f.*; silk —, corbata de
seda
tightly fuertemente
time tiempo *m.*, (*time that may be*
repeated) vez *f.*; hora *f.*; **at the**
same —, a la vez, al mismo
tiempo; **for a long** — **I have**
been looking for you hace
mucho (tiempo) que le busco a
Vd.; **from** — **to** —, de vez (cuando) en cuando; **have a good**
—, divertirse (ie) **102; what** —
is it? ¿ qué hora es ?; —**s:**
$2 \times 3 = 6$ dos por tres son seis

Tintoretto *Italian painter*

tocar (App. B, III, 1) touch; play (*musical instruments*)

todavía still, yet

todo, –a all; — lo bello (nuevo) everything beautiful (new); sobre —, above all, especially; —s los días every day

Toledo *former capital of Spain on the Tagus river*

tomar take

tomo *m.* volume, tome

torear fight (*in a bullfight*)

torero *m.* bullfighter

toril *m.* bullpen

toro *m.* bull ¡ a los —s ! to the bullfight! corrida de —s bullfight; plaza de —s bullring

torre *f.* tower

tortuoso, –a winding

trabajar work

traer 89 bring, carry

tranquilo, –a tranquil, calm, quiet

transparente transparent, clear

tratar treat; — de try to; —se de be a question of

trece thirteen

treinta thirty

tren *m.* train; ¡ señores viajeros al —! all aboard! bajar del —, get out of the train; subir al —, get on the train

tres three

tribunal *m.* court; — de las Aguas *court of justice at Valencia to deal with irrigation problems*

tristeza *f.* sadness

tumba *f.* tomb

turista *m.* tourist

ufano, –a proud

último, –a last

universidad *f.* university

un(o), –a a, an, one

unos, –as some, a few, about

útil useful

---

tired: be —, estar (16) cansado, –a; my eyes are —, tengo los ojos cansados

to a, para, de

tobacco store estanco *m.*

to-day hoy

to-morrow mañana *f.*; — morning mañana por la mañana

to-night esta noche

too demasiado; it is — hot hace demasiado calor; (= *also*) también

top (*floor, story*) último, –a

toward hacia

train tren *m.*

travel viajar

traveler viajero *m.*

treat tratarse de

tree árbol *m.*

trip viaje *m.*

trunk baúl *m.*

truth verdad *f.*

try (to) tratar (de)

Tuesday martes m.

turn volver (ue) 78

twelve doce

twenty veinte; — one veinte y un(o), veintiun(o)

two dos

umbrella paraguas *m.*

unable: be —, no poder 66

uncle tío *m.*; it is my —'s es de mi tío

understand comprender, entender (ie) (App. B, IV, 1)

unfortunately por desgracia

United States Estados Unidos

university universidad *f.*

unless a menos que, a no ser que

until hasta (que)

unwillingly de mala gama

up: get —, levantarse

us: to —, nos; (*after Spanish prep.*) nosotros, –as

use emplear, usar (de), servirse (de)

vacilar hesitate
Valencia *city and province in eastern Spain*
valenciano, -a Valencian
valer **144** be worth; — **la pena** be worth while
valor *m.* value
valle *m.* valley
Van Dyck, Anthony (1598–1641) *Flemish painter*
vapor *m.* steamer, steamship
varios, -as several
vaso *m.* glass
¡ vaya! well! indeed!
veinte y cuatro twenty-four
Velázquez, Diego (1599–1660) *celebrated Spanish painter*
vender sell
venir (a) **67** come
ventana *f.* window
ventanilla *f.* window (*in railway car or ticket office*)
ver (—) **87** see
verano *m.* summer
veras: de —, truly, really, in truth
verdad *f.* truth; es —, it is true
verdadero, -a true, real
vestidos *m. pl.* clothes
vestir (i) **116** dress; —se dress oneself; — de dress in

vez *f.* time; **a la** —, at the same time; **alguna** — ever, sometime; **de — en cuando** from time to time; **en — de** instead of
viajar travel; (el) —, traveling
viaje *m.* travel, trip; **en** — on the way; **hacer un** —, take a trip
viajero *m.* traveler; ¡ señores —s al tren! all aboard!
vida *f.* life
viejo, -a old
viento *m.* wind, hacer **(27)** —, be windy
vino *m.* wine
visita *f.* visit; **tarjeta de** — visiting card
visitar visit
vistoso, -a showy
vivamente ardently
vivir live
vivo, -a bright, vivid; **a lo** —, vividly
volver **78** return; volvió a hablar he spoke again
voz *f.* voice
vuelta *f.* return; billete de ida y — round-trip ticket; **estar (16) de** —, be back

Wáshington Washington

---

vaudeville variedades; *f. pl.* — show función de variedades; — **theater** teatro de variedades
verb verbo *m.*
very muy; — **much** mucho, muchísimo; **be** — **glad to** tener **(7)** mucho gusto en
virtue virtud *f*
visit visitar
volume tomo *m.*, volumen *m.*

wait esperar, aguardar
waiter mozo *m.*, camarero *m.*
wake (up) despertarse (ie) **88**
walk andar, caminar; **take a** — dar un paseo, ir a paseo, pasear(se)

want querer (—) **39**, desear (—)
warm caliente; (*weather*) be (very) —, hacer **(27)** (mucho) calor; (*personal*) tener **(7)** (mucho) calor
wash lavar; — **oneself** lavarse; **they** — **their faces** se lavan la cara
watch reloj *m.*
watchman sereno *m.*
water agua *f.*
wear llevar, traer **89**
weather tiempo *m.*; **be good (bad)** —, hacer **(27)** buen (mal) tiempo
Wednesday miércoles *m.*
week semana *f.*, ocho días

y and
ya already, now, finally
Yusuf I (1333-1354) *king of Granada*

---

well *adv.* bien; be —, estar (16)
bueno, –a (bien); — satisfied
muy satisfecho, –a
well! ¡ vaya! ¡ pues bien!
Wellington Wéllington
what *rel. pron.* lo que
what? ¿ qué? ¿ como? — is the
matter with you? ¿ qué tiene
Vd. ? ¿qué le pasa a Vd ?
what! ¡ qué! — a pity! ¡ qué lástima!
whatever (todo) lo que, cuanto, –a
when cuando
when ? ¿ cuándo ?
where donde, en donde, *(with
verb of motion)* a donde
where? ¿ dónde ? *(with verb of
motion)* ¿ a dónde ?
wherever donde, dondequiera
whew! ¡ cáspita!
which *rel. pron,* que, el que, etc.,
el cual, etc.
which ? ¿ cuál ?
while mientras; a little —, un
rato; a long —, mucho tiempo;
be worth —, valer (144) la pena
white blanco, –a
who *rel. pron.* que, el que, etc., el
cual, etc., quien *(see 122)*
who? ¿ quién ?
wholesale: at — al por mayor
whose cuyo, –a
whose? ¿ de quien ?
why? ¿ por qué ?
will (be willing) querer 39
willingly de buena gana
winding tortuoso, –a
window ventana *f.*, ventanilla *f.*
windy: be —, hacer (27) viento
wine vino *m.*
winter invierno *m.*
wish querer 39
with con, de; — me conmigo; what

zapato *m.* shoe
zarzuela *f.* musical comedy, comic
operetta

---

is the matter — you? ¿qué
tiene Vd. ? ¿ qué le pasa a Vd. ?
within dentro, *(prep.)* dentro de
without sin, *(conj.)* sin que
woman mujer *f.*
wonderful maravilloso, –a
word palabra *f.*
work trabajo *m.*, obra *f.*
work trabajar; — hard trabajar
mucho
working (el) trabajar
worn: be — out no poder (66) más
worth: be — (while)valer (la pena)
would that! ¡ ojalá ! ¡ ojalá que!
write escribir (Suppl. Ex. 1, C,
VIII)
written escrito, –a
wrong: be — no tener (7) razón

year año *m.*; a — ago hace un
año; be forty —s old tener (7)
cuarenta años
yellow amarillo, –a
yes sí
yesterday ayer
yet todavía, aun, *(after verb)* aún
you *(form.)* usted (Vd.), ustedes
(Vds.); *(fam.)* tú, vosotros, –as;
(dir. obj.) *(form.)* le, la, los, las,
(fam.) te, os; *(ind. obj.)* *(form.)*
le, les, *(fam.)* te, os; do — not?
¿ no es verdad ?
young joven
younger menor
your *(form.)* su(s), el de Vd., etc.,
(fam.) tu.(s); for — sake por Vd.
yours *(form.)* el suyo, etc., el de
Vd., etc., *(fam.)* el tuyo, etc.
yourself *(form.)* Vd. mismo, *(obj.
of verb)* se, *(obj. of prep.)* sí
youth juventud *f.*

zero cero *m.*

INDEX

[The numbers below refer to paragraphs.]

A

a, al (a + el), 1 (a); before direct object, 38, 38, footnotes 3 and 4, 120, footnote, 149, footnote; before infinitive, 166, and Appendix D.

acá, 108, footnote.

acabar, acabar de, 17, 17, footnote.

accentuation, Appendix A, I, diphthongs and triphthongs, II.

acostarse, conjugation, 134.

address, forms of, 72, 73.

adjectives, absolute superlative, 82, footnote; agreement, 23; apocopation, 25, 25, footnote; comparison, 82–85, inequality, 82–84, equality, 85, irregular, 83; replaces demonstrative pronoun, 111; with estar, 14; feminine, 22; used as nouns, 26; plural, 21; position, 24; with ser, 13; both with ser and estar, 14, footnote; sentence position of superlatives, 82, footnote; de for *in* after superlatives, 82, footnote; *see also* possessive, demonstrative, etc.

adverbs, comparison, 82–85, inequality, 82–84, equality, 85, irregular, 83; formed from adjectives, 86; lo used, 82, 3; aquí, acá, ahí, allí, allá, 108, footnote; mucho, 82–83; superlative, mucho, muy, 82, footnote; tan, 85, 92.

aficionado, ser aficionado a, 91.

ahí, 108, footnote.

al = a + el, 1 (a); followed by infinitive, 162, footnote; al contado, 176; al por mayor (menor), 177.

alguno, apocopation, 25; with negative value, 36, 1, footnote; algunos for unos, 1, footnote.

allá, 108, footnote.

allí, 108, footnote.

andar, conjugation, 54; with present participle, 169 (a).

antemano, de antemano, 147.

antes, cuanto antes, 92.

apocopation, 25, 25, footnote.

aquel, declension, 106, agreement and repetition, 107; meaning, 108.

aquél, declension, 106; use, 109; *the former*, 110; replaced by definite article, 111.

aquí, 108, footnote.

arithmetical signs, 62.

article, *see* definite and indefinite.

asir, conjugation, 173.

atención, prestar atención a, 138.

auxiliary verbs, *see* estar, haber, ser, tener.

B

bien, for bueno, 14, 1, footnote; comparison, 83; más bien, *rather*, 83, footnote.

bondad, tener la bondad de, 29.

bueno, apocopation, 25; comparison, 83; different meaning with ser or estar, 14, 1, footnote; de buena gana, 139.

but, pero, mas, sino, 36, 2; sino que, 36, 2, footnote; no ... sino or no ... más que, 36, 2 (a).

by, por, 113; de, 133, footnote.

C

caber, conjugation, 154.

caer, conjugation, 142.

can, poder and saber, 76, footnote.

-car verbs, Suppl. Ex. I, B; Appendix B, III, 1.

cardinals, table, 58; uses, 60; apocopation of uno, 25, of ciento, 25, footnote.

cargo, hacerse cargo de, 158.

castellano (el), used for *Spanish language*, 3, 6, footnote.

-cer verbs, Suppl. Ex. I, B; Appendix B, III, 2.

177

178 INDEX

[The numbers below refer to paragraphs.]

[The numbers below refer to paragraphs.]

184 INDEX